Contact Center Management

"By The Numbers"

by

Dr. Jon Anton
Director of Benchmark Research
Purdue University
Center for Customer-Driven Quality

and

Kamál Webb
Director of Benchmarking Practices
BenchmarkPortal, Inc.

Content Editor
John Chatterley
Director of Research
BenchmarkPortal, Inc.

Business Navigation

Only two centuries ago, early explorers (adventurous business executives of those bygone days) were guided primarily with a compass and celestial navigation using reference points like the North Star. Today's busy executive also needs guidance systems with just-in-time business intelligence to navigate through the challenges of locating, recruiting, keeping, and growing profitable customers. The Anton Press provides this navigational system through practical, how-to-do-it books for the modern day business executive.

ISBN 0-9761109-0-3

Dedication

I dedicate this book to all those contact center professionals that manage Purdue University certified "Centers of Excellence." These managers have truly balanced their performance to be both very effective and very efficient. In visiting these certified world-class centers, I have met the talented managers who taught me all their secrets of "managing by the numbers." This book is an anthology of everything that they taught me over the years.

Jon Anton

I would like to dedicate this book to the loving memory of my parents, Hiram and Gloria, whom always believed in me; to my wife, Jin-Hee, who has stood by me regardless; and to my children, my son, Berkely, and my daughters Alexzena and Lynn who are a source of constant inspiration.

Kamál Webb

Table of Contents

List of Figures

ACKNOWLEDGEMENTS

I want to acknowledge the hard work and dedication of my co-author, Kamal Webb, in the research and writing of this book. I have known Kamal for years and during that time we have talked about this book on many occasions. The fact is, many professionals "talk about writing a book." Some even begin writing, but never finish the effort. In my experience, only a very few have the perseverance and dedication, and are willing to sacrifice their discretionary time to actually complete a book. Kamal was that driving force of talent, energy, and determination to ferret through the many dead-ends to help us complete this book in a timely fashion. He is a wonderful friend (both personal and professional), and now an established co-author.

Jon Anton

One of the most famous quotes of all times is of President John F. Kennedy who said: "Ask not what your country can do for you, but what you can do for your country." Today, however, we live in a global society where businesses support customers in all faces of the world. The most dynamic representation of this is the contact center. Contact centers connect both businesses to other businesses, businesses to their employees (the help desk), and businesses to their customer's worldwide. Therefore, the jobs of contact center professionals, like pieces of a jigsaw puzzle, have a direct impact on the global community. This book is designed to provide contact center professionals with the insights and tools necessary to guide their centers into optimal practices and compete in an ever-advancing global community efficiently and effectively.

I would first and foremost like to thank Dr. Jon Anton, a pioneer in contact center best and optimal practices, for his patience, kindness, and willingness to serve as my mentor and most valuable critic over the past four years and for his trust and confidence in me to assist him in the re-write of the original form of this book. Single-handedly, Dr. Anton has brought contact centers to the forefront of the modern business model; developed and inspired systems whereby

ix

contact center professionals can accurately monitor and measure the operations of their centers, discovered new best practices, and refaced the customer experience in contact center at a global level.

I would like to acknowledge the many managers whom have shared their data and participated in our benchmarking studies at BenchmarkPortal, with special recognition to managers Craig Smith, Toni Roberts, and Rita Parker who have put to practice and proved valid our theories and suggestions, and moreover, have become good friends in the process.

I would also like to add special thanks Michael Feinberg as a source of constant encouragement and John Chatterley for his many years of support, guidance, and friendship.

Kamál Webb

And finally, we both wish to thank our production team, including Debi Cloud, Susan Hampton, and Brenda Williams, for their very professional work in taking our numerous drafts of the manuscript, and transforming its many words, graphs, and tables into an attractive and readable book.

By

Joe Mangiaracina
Vice President, Customer Relationship Management
Broadview Networks
a Purdue University "Center of Excellence"

With the ever increasing complexity of multi-channel customer contact handling, it is significant that this is the first book to address the challenges of managing such a contact center comprised of customer service agents, documented workflow processes, and enabling technology.

The authors have written a very practical guide to managing a customer contact center "by the numbers." In contrast to most other departments in a company, the contact center has a constant flow of available performance metrics that are critical for the manager to use in making real-time decisions. The challenge is always what action to take when the "numbers change," and what remedies are best suited for specific performance gaps.

In my 20 years of experience in designing, implementing, re-engineering, and managing world-class customer contact centers, I have tried many different management styles and techniques. The following "Baker's Dozen" of critical success factors are my favorites:

1. Anticipate issues, don't wait for the worst to happen.

2. Use internal and external (voice of customer) performance metrics to give you early warnings of trends both positive and negative.

3. Know how gaps in performance are quantified, and how big the gap must be before you act.

4. Understand when a gap implicates a specific contact center process that needs your attention and management action.

5. Be sure your entire staff and employees understand the numbers that are critical to success and share these numbers daily with your team.

6. Benchmark your performance with other contact centers with similar challenges to see how you stack up.

7. Constantly measure, plan for change, implement the change, then measure the impact, then begin the cycle all over again.

8. Set realistic performance goals based upon your past performance and best practices as established by a peer group.

9. Constantly balance effectiveness (quality) with efficiency (quantity).

10. Make sure you balance performance metrics that you are using to guide your management of the contact center with the "voice of the customer."

11. Make sure every individual from the front-line agent to the top managers have quantitative goals to self-manage their own hourly, daily, weekly, monthly, and yearly performance.

12. Develop a compensation system based on quantitative performance metrics, i.e., reward "by the numbers."

13. Implement your own "dashboard" of key performance indicators (KPIs), and guide you contact center "by the numbers."

In this book, the authors touch on all the important management tools needed to achieve world-class performance in a customer service contact center. Today's contact center managers need to balance people, process and technology in order to achieve "World Class" performance. Numbers are only numbers, its what you do with them that counts. Your decision-making should be based on facts and not emotion, however, you must balance the human aspect of what you are doing as this is a people business and the interaction that customers, distributors, and suppliers have with your organization is critical to the success of the overall enterprise. The contact center manager's job is never done. You can't ever relax or declare victory as every activity in the organization eventually impacts the contact center and vice versa. Use your performance metrics to educate other divisions in your company and get their buy-in to your success as well as theirs. Lastly, celebrate successes and let the rest of the organization know the value that you deliver to the company. I know you will enjoy the book and find it very useful in improving your management style and effectiveness. Best of Luck.

Background

The task of maintaining quality customer service and obtaining customer satisfaction has become a measured science. With the addition of multimedia access channels like e-mail, the Internet, and an array of Web services to a new wave of customer relationship strategies, the traditional contact center has evolved into a customer contact center that is sophisticated, automated and technologically superior to the call center (see figure 1). Customers who once called the traditional AGENT-intensive inbound call center are now greeted by interactive voice response (IVR) units, computer telephony integration (CTI), or may access the contact center through a variety of self-service Web applications.

Although these new customer contact centers have become the focal point of technological advancements aimed at interfacing businesses with their customers through electronic media in addition to the telephone, the importance and functionality that they share with their predecessor, the call center, remains highly similar and equally noteworthy:

- The customer contact center is still the most proactive method to differentiate companies and their products.

- Customers are no longer satisfied with having only one traditional method of contact, the toll-free number. They anticipate, and even demand, seamless access to quick and efficient customer service by companies on any day, at any time, by keyboard as well as by phone.

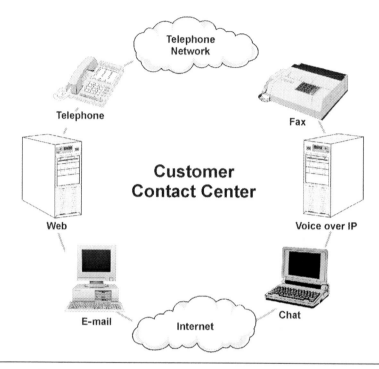

Figure 1. Diagram of a typical customer contact center

Moreover, with the rising cost of technology and a greater corporate awareness to satisfy stakeholder interests, contact centers are looked by corporate management for their ability to create new revenue sources, and promote customer retention. Budgets for contact centers, which have multiplied in size, are balanced upon the contact center being either a corporate asset or liability.

In the modern corporate business model of customer service strategy, management of the contact center is mission critical to the success of customer support. Management of the contact center has moved from a reactive "fire-fighting" style to a more proactive tactical style of professional management. Measurements drive behavior, and "you get what you measure and reward." The primary purpose of this book is to provide new professional and contact center managers with a methodology for "managing their contact centers by the numbers."

The technology of today's contact center presents the potential of generating an enormous array of data for use by contact center managers and professionals. Specialized software packages process the data into useful metrics and then organize it for presentation into formatted graphs and charts. This permits management at three different levels:

1. The contact service agent (CSR) level
2. The supervisor of agents level
3. The contact center as a department entity

It is not at all intuitively obvious how to relate contact center metrics to required management action. What do these contact center metrics mean to the various process managers, such as those in Telecommunications and Human Resources, who support or impact the contact center's performance? For instance, what does it mean if the caller abandon rate increased this month, and what should be done about it? If agent talk time goes down by 3%, should we take action? If "yes," who should do what?

Contact centers, like other businesses, have an obligation to their stakeholders to provide a reasonable service at a reasonable cost, yet still be competitive. How can companies do this without knowing at what point being good is "good enough" to satisfy its business needs as well as the demands of its customers?

In businesses that take in millions of calls per year over their toll-free telephone numbers, the affect of just one-half minute per call can be astounding. Let us see how this figures. On an average, most companies pay around seven cents per minute for their toll-free line. Therefore, if Company A's call center receives an average of only 1.5 million calls annually, with an average talk time of 4.5 minutes per call, they are spending a yearly average of $472,500 ($.07 x 6,750,000 minutes) just for toll charges. This cost does not include the hourly wage of the agent or other operating expenses incurred.

Let us now compare this to the average talk time of Company A's industry peers, which is only three minutes per call, with the same volume of calls per year, and with the same toll charge per minute. At first glance, what could the difference of a simple minute and a half make? Although the numbers of calls were the same, the minutes dropped considerably, to 4.5 million. This reduced the phone bill to $315,000, a savings of $157,500, as illustrated in figure 2.

	Company A	Industry Peers	Gap	% Gap
Cost Per Minute	$0.07	$0.07	$0.00	0.00%
Annual Call Volume	1,500,000	1,500,000	0	0.00%
Average Talk Time (in minutes/call)	4.50	3.00	1.50	33.33%
Annual Toll Cost	$472,500	$315,000	$157,500	33.33%

Figure 2. The simple gap

The issue becomes crystal-clear. There is an obvious performance gap between Company A and its peers who are doing the same work, but more efficiently, and probably more effectively! This gap, now represented by dollars, is a cost to the stakeholders of the company.

To maintain the competitive edge, managers must find a way to create a balance between the efficient and effective operation of the contact center and avoid serious performance gaps with their peers.

With the modern business model providing customers with multiple access channels for customer contact, including telephone, e-mail, and Web access points, these channels of customer contact must be clearly understood and managed appropriately.

This document is designed to assist the contact center manager and supervisors in getting behind the numbers to see what actions make sense given changes that occur to the contact center metrics. In doing so, we rely heavily on the following:

1. Cutting-edge telecommunications and information technology to generate the internal metrics

2. A cooperative and efficient accounting department to supply financial data

3. A state-of-the-art external caller satisfaction (CS) program to amplify the voice of the caller

4. An understanding of each customer contact channel and access point

5. An understanding of the value that the customer brings to the contact center

With these, and the skill and knowledge to analyze the data, we will demonstrate how to make the numbers yield the information that is needed for management to formulate tactical plans and make strategic decisions. In addition to this, you will be able to constantly focus on first being more effective in delivering what the caller needs, and second on being more efficient and cost-effective in delivering world-class customer service through the contact center.

Additionally, we will indicate how process managers can make use of the contact center data and which process managers probably need to supply the contact center with more information. Moreover, we will show how drilling down through certain high-level metrics to examine their supporting numbers is one key method, by which a manager can "manage by the numbers."

We define contact center management as "the effective management of the right number of full time equivalents (FTEs) to ensure that callers experience the highest quality of service at the right time and every time."

Managing the Contact Center to a Mission

Understanding the tactical mission of the contact center in the overall scope and direction of the corporation's business strategy is the most critical and important first step in developing a contact center measurement and management approach. The fundamental goals of "Centers of Excellence" are to:

- reduce costs
- get new customers
- keep existing customers
- grow profitable customers

The business challenges for contact centers include:

- achieving maximum efficiency and effectiveness of their operations
- developing cross-channel integration
- shifting from a cost-focus to a profit-focus

What every CEO wants is:

- decreased costs (Efficiency)
- increased revenues (Profits)
- increased customer satisfaction (Effectiveness)
- increased wallet-share (Loyalty)
- increased market-share (Knowledge)

In 2000, it is estimated that there were over 15 billion customer contacts made to contact centers, with the majority of contacts via the telephone, as shown in figure 3 below:

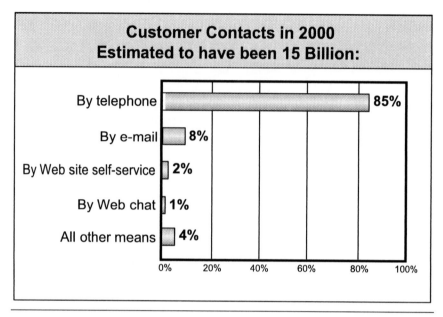

Figure 3. Customer contacts in 2000

By 2005, the estimated number of customer contacts is projected to expand to over 30 billion contacts, with much of this growth being channeled through alternative contact points, as illustrated in figure 4.

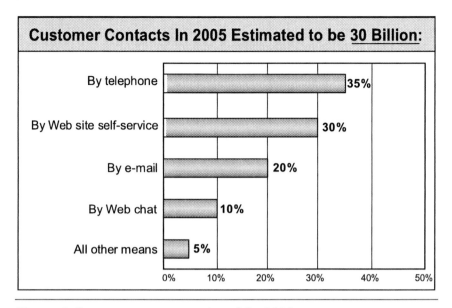

Figure 4. Customer contacts projected for 2005

The CRM Vision

The global marketplace is an amazing and complex place today. Competition for market share grows exponentially with each passing moment as business is conducted at the speed of the Internet— instantly! While customer relationship management (CRM) has been around for a quarter of a century, the growing expectations of customers is pushing technology companies to add new capabilities to serve customers faster, better, and with more satisfaction. It can be very confusing to a technology buyer to determine what is needed to provide true customer relationship management.

Today, customer-facing businesses are at a critical point in their development, but many do not realize it. The twin challenges of CRM and multi-channel customer contact have emerged. Neither can be ignored, but both create risks of their own. By the end of 2004, over $150 billion will have been spent on CRM-enabling technologies. Most of this will be wasted due to lack of planning, undefined business goals, and the absence of measurement.

According to Gartner research, "Through 2004, 55% of CRM initiatives will fail to meet measurable benefit objectives and will fail to positively affect return on investment, due to lack of business processes for conducting ongoing measurements." *(Source: Gartner, "In Pursuit of CRM Economics")*

CRM is not a technology, or even a group of technologies. It is a continually evolving process which requires a shift in attitude away from the traditional business model of focusing internally. CRM is an approach a company takes towards its customers, backed up by thoughtful investment in people, technology, and business processes.

The concept of CRM contains everything that all businesses need to succeed:

- **Customer**: All businesses, when they first start, have to focus on the needs of their customers. As businesses grow and become more complex, they become more inward looking as they try to cope with their internal issues. Often, the customer gets treated as an afterthought. With CRM, one goal is to make the individual customer become important once again at an acceptable cost to the company.

- **Relationship**: Until recently, it was impossible for large companies to form relationships with customers. With a customer base of millions, how can a company know their individual preferences or dislikes? This is an area where technology can help businesses build lasting relationships with customers, to keep them loyal and increase their value to the company.

- **Management**: Realistically, businesses are not implementing CRM because they have had a change of heart and decided to be nice to the long-suffering customer. Loyalty equals profit! Both the customer and the company benefit from it. The "management" part of CRM demonstrates that it is the business which ultimately controls the relationship with the customer:
  - it provides the right information at the right time
  - it offers the right price to keep the customer happy enough to stay
  - it anticipates what else the customer would like to buy, and understands why

The business objective of CRM is to maximize profit from customers, as a result of knowing them, treating them well, and fulfilling their needs.

Through our research, we have found that about 50% of a contact center manager's responsibility is ensuring that customer contacts are responded to in a timely and professional manner, while the other 50% is reporting back to the corporation about the customer's needs and how to address them. This balance is not often understood, so corrective action is not implemented.

Furthermore, it is essential that the mission of the contact center be aligned with the corporate business strategy. For instance, the following three contact center types would have substantially different measurement and management approaches:

1. A high volume, navigational contact center is designed to give simple answers and quickly re-route the caller to a more appropriate individual depending on the nature of the call.

2. A revenue-producing contact center's primary purpose is order taking and pre-sales consultation.

3. A customer care contact center is designed to provide immediate support, and its main purpose is to assist the customer after the sale and build a long-term relationship. This includes, but is not limited to, the technical support center.

Formulating a consistent business strategy for a contact center requires synchronized planning to achieve multiple and sometimes competing objectives. The typical business objectives that might drive a contact center include:

1. Delighting the caller into a mindset of loyalty and preference

2. Optimizing organizational imperatives

3. Implementing cultural values

4. Maximizing the existing technological environment

5. Working within the human resource capability profile

6. Optimizing operational strategy and process efficiency

The following are several questions that should be asked of any contact center management approach:

1. Is the approach effective for managing the integration of multiple technologies?

2. Is the approach effective for analyzing customer behavior to maximize value?

3. Is the approach effective for providing management with the information to make effective decisions?

4. Is the approach effective for measuring staff performance?

5. Is the approach effective for improving customer problem resolution speed?

6. Is the approach effective for understanding and acting upon caller satisfaction or dissatisfaction issues?

In this book, we have chosen to implement a singular business strategy that can cut across all contact centers, regardless of their real or implied business objective, and that strategy is to "delight" your callers into a mindset of loyalty and preference. Research conducted by both corporate and academic researchers shows a relationship between survey measurements and the degree of preference or rejection that a customer might have accumulated. When the customer is asked a customer satisfaction question, the customer's degree of loyalty mindset (or attitude) will be indicated as a score from 1 (very dissatisfied) to 5 (very satisfied).

Figure 5 shows the non-linearity of the relationship between satisfaction and loyalty. Overlaid on this curve are the approximate areas where the customer goes from rejection to acceptance to preference. (Obviously, the goal of every company is to develop customer relationships to a level of high preference; i.e., we all want the coveted preferred vendor status such that when the customer is given a choice, the result will be that your firm is selected every time.)

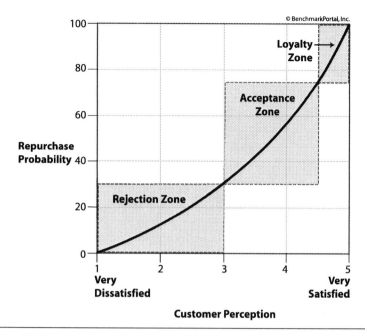

Figure 5. The relationship between loyalty and performance

It is interesting to note that a very satisfied customer is almost six times more likely to be loyal and to repurchase and/or to recommend your product than a customer who is just satisfied.

In subsequent chapters of this book, we will define a level of customer delight, based on our research, as a Customer Satisfaction Index (CSI) = 85. This measure allows you to achieve loyalty without spending extra time or money beyond that needed for a high probability of customer retention. The key is to reach a level of caller satisfaction with a sufficiently high probability of customer retention at a cost that is within the established budget of your contact center.

Figure 6 is a model of how "managing by the numbers" should fit into a total contact center management process. Note that "managing by the numbers" is accomplished via input from external metrics (i.e., the caller satisfaction or CSI index data referred to in figure 5), competitor contact centers (i.e., best-in-class benchmarking data), and internal metrics (i.e., average speed of answer, percent abandoned calls and the like). Information from these three sources combined in a management process leads to quality management decisions.

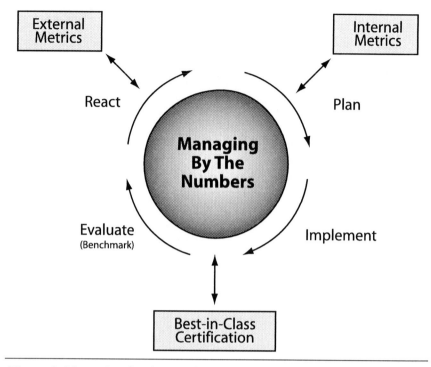

Figure 6. Managing by the numbers

What Do People Who Contact Our Centers Expect From Us?

Questions we might ask up front are "What is a quality phone call," or "What constitutes a quality service via e-mail?" From our experience and research in over 1,500 contact centers, the following elements make up a quality phone call that will have a high probability of resulting in a delighted caller contact:

1. The caller did not get a busy signal

2. The caller was not forced to wade through a myriad of IVR menus in order to gain proper assistance

3. The caller was not placed on hold for too long

4. The call was answered without holding, transferring, or calling back

5. All answers were accurate

6. The agent captured all needed and useful information from the caller quickly and accurately

7. The caller was not rushed off the phone

8. The caller developed confidence in the agent

9. Unsolicited marketplace feedback was detected, acted upon, and an unexpected suggestion made to the caller

10. The caller did not feel it necessary to check-up, verify, or repeat the call

11. The agent had pride in workmanship such that they behaved like a professional

The following elements make up a quality e-mail exchange that will have a high probability of resulting in a delighted e-customer contact:

1. The e-customer was not forced to wait a prolonged time in order to receive a response

2. The response received was worded in a clear, understandable and concise language

3. The e-mail response used proper grammar and did not contain spelling errors

4. Links to other helpful sources of information were supplied

5. Additional access points were provided for advanced support options

Because our goal is building a world-class contact center measurement and management information system that constantly focuses on re-engineering the customer's contact with the center to increase the probability of caller delight, we should briefly summarize the typical caller expectations as determined from our research. We have found that customers who contact centers have very predictable and similar requirements across industries, products, and services. Some of these requirements follow:

1. Be accessible

2. Treat me courteously

3. Be responsive to what I need and want

4. Do what I ask of you promptly

5. Don't make me deal with poorly trained and ill-informed agents

6. Do it right the first time

7. Follow up as promised

8. Tell me what to expect

9. Be honest

10. Be socially responsible

11. Be ethical

12. Remember me the next time I contact you

As customer access points develop and become increasingly diverse (telephone, e-mail, Web-services, etc.), the customer concept of a prompt response and quality customer service also changes accordingly. Varied tolerances develop for each level of service that a contact center provides. Six factors combine to form caller tolerance:

1. The degree of motivation is illustrated in willingness to wait to talk to your doctor when you're sick compared to willingness to wait to make an airline reservation.

2. The availability of substitutes is the ease of obtaining the same product or service elsewhere.

3. The competition's service level impacts the level of service you must provide just to stay competitive.

4. The level of caller expectations, which may partially be based on demographics, sets the caller's level of anticipated service. For example, New York callers abandon three times more quickly than Phoenix callers.

5. The time available to the caller, or lack thereof, due to current circumstances such as need to catch a plane.

6. Toll costs to the caller, such as whether the call is a 1-900 versus a 1-800 number call.

We focus our attention on three key qualities of service measures in this book:

1. What are caller expectations?

2. Are we meeting them?

3. Are we using the fewest possible company resources to achieve a sufficient level of caller satisfaction to ensure customer retention?

Setting the Service Levels to Achieve Caller Delight

In subsequent chapters we will describe a methodology to establish service levels that correlate to caller delight. In addition, the optimum service levels should be affected by these inputs:

1. The financial value of the call

2. Local agent labor costs

3. Local trunk line costs

4. The six factors of caller tolerance previously listed

5. The company's desire to differentiate products or services by the level of service provided in the contact center

6. Alternate customer contact points

Attributes Of A Successful Contact Center Manager

A contact center manager is a unique new professional that has combined skills in human resources, budgeting, information technology, telecommunications, and statistics to name only a few. The job now requires someone who is not only adept with great people skills, but understands the new technology of the industry. The following attributes characterize most successful contact center managers:

1. They have aligned their contact center mission with the corporate mission.

2. They have learned that the contact center's tactical strategy must stem from their company's business strategy.

3. They understand the incoming contact center as a total, interrelated, and integrated set of processes.

4. They understand that contact center management requires ready access to specific internal and external measurements.

5. They emphasize quality of service over quantity of service.

6. They constantly strive for forecasting accuracy.

7. They recognize the value of training.

8. They are doing something specific about agent turnover.

9. They know the key contact center metrics and understand the simple statistical routines to analyze improvement.

10. They know that selling their budget to senior management means speaking in management terminology and properly addressing financial issues in terms of return on investment and customer lifetime value in dollars and cents.

11. They are willing to experiment to improve and even re-engineer each process.

12. They take the initiative in coordinating with other departments.

13. They use the contact center to conduct valuable customer research.

What happens when caller expectations are not met and delight is not established? To demonstrate this, we will look at how "queue time" influences both customer service and caller satisfaction. Queue time, as you may recall, is one of the customer satisfaction KPIs mentioned earlier.

A simple example of queue time is that amount of time a caller waits for assistance after pressing "1" for the next available agent, after calling a customer service number for assistance. The customer never sees the back-end operation, and only realizes that they are waiting for something that they feel should be instantaneous. As the caller waits, tension mounts, and the caller becomes agitated or disgruntled. When finally greeted by the agent, it becomes the natural reaction for the customer to lodge a complaint.

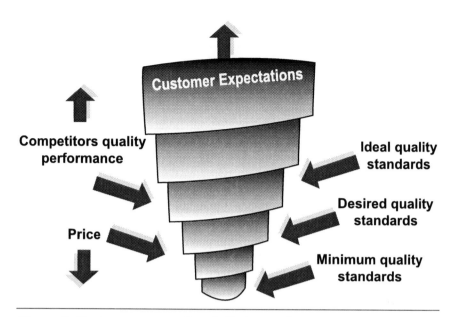

Figure 7. Customer expectations inflation cycle

Unfortunately in most cases, the agent has little recourse but to listen compassionately. This however can also have a negative effect on the agent, who may later treat other customers with a less than caring attitude. But what was responsible for the delay which caused the customer to wait? We find that there may be many reasons.

A primary factor for long queue times (in excess of one-minute), is agent staffing. This alludes that the contact center does not employ enough people to handle the incoming calls. The fact may be however, that there are a sufficient number of agents employed, just not available. This is when the question of adherence to schedule comes into play; are the agents in their seats and available to take calls when needed? Agents need to be in their seats and available to take calls.

Other queue building factors are technology-related issues such as skill based routing and training. Not having enough agents available, who are skilled and trained with the knowledge to resolve the call, creates a bottleneck that often results in high queue times. The resulting effect of these combined issues is a vortex, which continuously pulls at the fabric of business to consumer relations and diminishes customer satisfaction. To combat this, companies need to develop a focused approach towards the establishment of best practices for the contact center. Success only comes from management focused on engineering caller experiences that produce delight.

Corporate Image versus Financial Performance

The performance of a company's contact center can have either a very positive or a very negative effect on the corporate image as perceived by customers. With contact center costs skyrocketing, many executives are questioning whether these expenditures are warranted even if the result is improved corporate image and customer goodwill.

The question "Does the public image of a corporation affect the volume of sales of its products or services?" was put to the test in recent research conducted at Purdue University's Center for Customer-Driven Quality and BenchmarkPortal. Although the research is still ongoing, initial results reported that in 80% of the Fortune 1,000 companies studied, the qualitative measure of image is a statistically significant leading indicator of the direction of the next year's sales volume. See Appendix G for more details on this research project.

Outline of This Book

Chapter 1 has provided an overview of recent important changes in the contact center industry with emphasis on the criticality of delighting callers. The foundation of caller expectations and a discussion of setting optimum service levels followed. Finally we indicated the characteristics of successful contact center managers.

In Chapter 2 we set out to determine the value of a caller. We rest our case largely on the concept of customer lifetime value (CLV), and explain how to compute it.

In Chapter 3 we lay out the key internal metrics, provide definitions as well as data capture and reporting frequencies, indicate cross-industry averages and suggest goal ranges, and indicate the managerial actions most likely required depending on changes in the metrics. Naturally, we cannot hope to account for all eventualities, and each organization will be run somewhat differently; but the generalities we cover should provide a solid basis for appropriate action in the contact center.

In Chapter 4 we present a proven model of the caller satisfaction measurement process as a way to determine and track external metrics, and in Chapter 5 we link internal and external metrics together.

Chapter 6 discusses the benefits of benchmarking your contact center as a means of determining the efficiency and effectiveness of your center's operation compared with industry best practices. This chapter also presents the concept of continuous improvement and contact center certification.

Chapter 7 takes the reader through a return on investment adaptation and provides a detailed example of the computation of this important ratio. The rationale for its use is developed as a means of measuring the performance of the contact center as a part of the overall enterprise. To enhance the undertaking of the ROI calculation, we develop an extended case study in which a 1% change is traced through the calculations to yield the final ROI.

In Chapter 8, the spectrum of workforce management and measurement is explored in depth, including the impact of culture and change management on the workforce, as well as the benefits and drawback of various workforce management approaches.

Chapter 9 covers quality monitoring and coaching in the contact center, including best practices and key performance indicators (KPIs) related to the quality monitoring and coaching process.

Chapter 10 explores an emerging aspect of contact center management, that paying attention to your agents and making them feel part of something bigger than just a row of computer stations is key to your success.

Some organizations provide rewards and penalties to their agents based solely on internal metrics such as number of calls handled, talk time, hold time, and transfers. This method of compensation is deaf to the voice of the caller.

In Chapter 11 we suggest a more complete incentive program based on linking internal and external metrics.

In addition, this book includes an updated glossary and a collection of appendices that expand upon the performance indicators, concepts and practices discussed in the chapters, and offers sample caller satisfaction surveys, internal surveys, and benchmarking questionnaires.

Corporate executives always seem to have a professional fixation on their company's income statement and balance sheet. For some, it's almost an obsession. They keep score and measure their performance by the gains in corporate assets and the rising value of stock. Since most executives also receive bonuses based on these financial scores, it's little wonder that they focus on these results.

Uniquely, the most important corporate asset, and the one with the greatest lasting value—loyal customers—isn't even reported by most companies. In fact, a research project conducted at Purdue University (Anton, 1994) reviewed the annual reports of all publicly-owned Fortune 500 companies and found no record of customer satisfaction trends or even numbers of loyal and dedicated customers. The most important asset was often not even mentioned.

Therefore, the values of customers or even the number of loyal customers are not typically issues of focal concern to executives or managers. Yet we would argue that little could be of more importance in this highly competitive world. Customer loyalty is even more important in volatile industries such as financial services, telecommunications, consumer electronics, and computers. Loyal customers are typically inclined to:

- buy more
- increase the frequency of purchases
- establish you as a preferred vendor
- encourage others to buy your products and services
- buy other products and services that you offer

Defining Customer Lifetime Value (CLV)

So, what is the real value of a customer? It is the lifetime value realized from the revenue stream that each customer brings to the company. That is, most customers change vendors infrequently, and many stay for years with the same firm. When a customer is gained or saved through customer service, it is not only the revenues generated in one month or one year that are the value to the company; rather it is the present value of the future stream of revenues generated from that customer for as long as the customer remains loyal.

This is the only truly valid measure of the value of a customer to a firm. We have developed a method for computing the lifetime value of a customer by simply borrowing from existing financial concepts and models, which are easily recognized by any company's accounting department.

Calculating Customer Lifetime Value (CLV)

The connection between a successful CRM operation and customer profitability is the value of customers "saved" from leaving the company. When a customer is gained or saved through customer service, the value of the customer is the present value of the future streams of revenue from that customer for as long as the customer remains with the company. In order to convert the number of saved customers to customer profitability, the customer lifetime value of the customer is calculated. The method for computing the CLV uses existing and proven financial concepts and models.

One Customer's Value

For the sake of illustration, we will demonstrate a customer lifetime value calculation assuming for one customer that:

1. The stream of revenues from the customer is level across time at $25 per month or $300 per year $= R$

2. The interest rate (opportunity cost) is the bank rate paid on the money for which no other specific use is made and is assumed to be 9% $= i$

3. The time a typical customer stays with a company (unique to this example) is 3 years $= n$

4. The formula for the calculation is then:

$$CLV = \frac{R \left(1 - \left[\frac{1}{(1+i)^n}\right]\right)}{i}$$

Where:

$R =$ annual revenue received from a loyal customer

$i =$ the relevant interest rate or opportunity cost of money per period.

$n =$ the number of periods in which a customer makes purchases

Using a month's revenue from the average customer, we have the R of the equation above. For the sake of making a calculation, $25 a month times 12 or $300 a year will be assumed as the revenue from the average customer.

The opportunity cost of money (i) is different for every company. At the minimum, it should be the interest rate the organization would be paid if the money were put to no other use; i.e., the rate a bank would pay if the money were on deposit. For the sake of illustration here, 9% will be assumed as the opportunity cost of money.

Annuities are generally calculated on the annual receipts of moneys paid at the end of each year. There is nothing, however, to keep these periods from being months rather than years so long as the opportunity cost of money is translated to a monthly rather than an annual interest rate and the annual periods are converted to months. To keep it simple, our calculations here will make the standard finance assumptions of an annual annuity paid at the end of the year.

But the real issue relative to the number of periods is not whether periods should be months or years; rather it is how many years the customer is likely to be with the company (therefore, the origin of the term customer lifetime), for that will allow the calculation of the true value of a customer saved today. If the average customer lifetime is available, it is simply a matter of having the computer calculate the longevity of the average customer.

Basically, your average customer lifetime value can be determined empirically, and may actually be known by your sales or accounting departments. We suggest you partner with these departments to make the final CLV determination more realistic.

For the purpose of our example here, three years will be assumed as the length of time the average customer stays with the company. Note that the implication is that a delighted caller is saved for another three-year period in addition to whatever length of time that customer has already been with the company.

Based on the foregoing assumptions, the calculation can now be made as follows:

$$CLV = \frac{300 \; (1 - \left[\dfrac{1}{(1 + .09)^3}\right])}{.09}$$

In our example, the lifetime value profitability of our typical customer is $759.39. Calculating the value of a saved customer is identical to calculating the lifetime value profitability. Why? With everything else being equal, a customer saved can be expected to stay another lifetime.

More Than One Customer and Customer Segment's Values

Once you have the sense of how to calculate this for one customer, you can then look at larger groups. The first step is to take a select group of customers that were acquired at about the same time and determine how many are still with your company a year later. This will give you your customer retention value. You can then compute the revenue generated by this set of customers by taking the above formula and multiplying it by the number of customers with this type of buying history. This gives you the value of that particular customer segment. The calculation can be repeated for other customer segments with different buying histories and customer lifetime values. With each of the calculations, it will become clear which segments provide the most value and where you want to focus your efforts.

Customer Appreciation through Customer Lifetime Value (CLV)

It is from understanding the value of your customers; you can then begin to look at how they provide an added value to managing your contact center. This allows you to differentiate between the non-beneficial customer, and the loyal and life-long core customers (see figure 8).

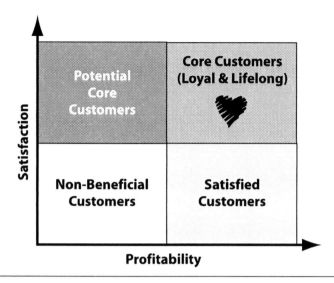

Figure 8. Customer differentiation and contribution to profitability

Furthermore, an understanding of the CLV of your customers allows you to ask the following questions about your current management practices:

- Where would your ROI come from?
- What are you measuring?
- What are you missing?
- How many customers use more than one product?
- What is my customer retention rate?
- Are you cross-selling the customer on other products?
- In what ways can customer service be improved?
- Are you maintaining the competitive market share?

The key points behind understanding CLV are to evaluate the profit that the customer brings to the company, be able to strategize for customer growth, and improve on those processes that will lead to increased communications, connectivity, and sales with the customer, thus optimizing the customer life cycle.

Increasing Corporate Customer Assets

Once you understand the value of your customers, you can then begin to look at how they provide value and add that to the above calculations. You'll want to look at:

- Where would your ROI come from?

- What are you measuring?

- What are you missing?

- Are you measuring adoption-resistance to the technology implementation?

- Are you factoring in implementation and rework costs of the technology because the customer doesn't know how to use the system properly?

> "In many instances, companies spend millions of dollars on CRM systems, only to find out that a $12/hour call center agent is not really using the new case management system. Adoption resistance exits because change management and a proper way to manage service levels are left out of the equation."
> —Lisa Schwartz, Co-author of *Change Management In Technology Implementations: Reducing the Risks of Failures*

You don't want your success to depend on variables that are controllable but go untouched because they don't seem like they will have a financial impact. In Section 6 we examine CRM project risk management and ways to decrease the extra financial expenditures that arise when this is not built into the implementation.

When the financial aspects of CRM systems are considered, sometimes the expected return is to recoup the actual costs of CRM deployment. To obtain the maximum return and increase the value of a customer, you'll want to strategize on how you want the customer to increase profits. The following list will give you some ideas how customers can add value through the CRM system:

1. The customer's use of one product

2. Cross-selling the customer on other products

3. Direct efficiency savings pay for deployment

4. Retaining customers

5. Cross-selling

6. Up-selling

7. Being more competitive

8. Improve e-customer service

9. Sales force automation

10. Improved sales process communications and connectivity—increasing leads, closings and retention

11. Increase customer life cycle—marketing, sales, service cycle

12. Analytics optimization—finding customers and products that are the most profitable mix

In addition, you want to understand that when purchasing CRM software, when ROI is promised, how much of the functionality of the CRM solution needs to be used to obtain that.

A good example is, for instance, Microsoft Word™. It is the word processing software that most people use to create documents. It is certainly faster and more efficient than using a typewriter. However, of the functional power of the software, how much of it do you use? It is very powerful, but many people don't use half of the functions it can provide: equation maker, footnotes, fancy tables, etc.

The idea here is to examine all the full functionalities of using a CRM system, and then to determine what it is that you are actually using and how to increase the cost benefit of having it. And how much functionality did you pay for, how much are you using and how much ROI are you getting out of it?

Adoption Resistance and Rework—Debts

Part of the reason many technology companies that sell CRM systems don't experience the true profits they might expect is that they spend their profits to solve "adoption resistance" and do re-work. You probably have calculated what it costs to develop and deliver the software/hardware. You may have added what you need for a margin to make a profit. But have you figured in the cost of re-work?

Re-work is when the client comes back and says, "The software doesn't do what you said. We tried ten times and get the same thing." You know that it is the user, but in order to really verify the problem, you have to go back to your engineers and ask them to look into this and figure out what the customer doesn't understand. This may take the time of sales people, marketing people, and C-level executives to smooth over the situation. Those people's time spent on re-work costs the company money. In some cases, it might be that there is a glitch that needs fixing, and that leads into a whole other cost situation.

Multiply the salaries of the people by the number of hours they spend after the sale. Then add the time that they didn't spend on new projects and the potential loss of revenue if they were selling to another customer. This is a double hit.

Other costs are market damage that we calculate in the next section, as well as the cost of bad word of mouth—i.e., loss of future sales because the CEOs of companies golf together and tell each other: "Don't buy XZY system because...." All these factors need to be considered when calculating ROI of CRM technology. Basically companies selling technology are often spending their profits in adoption re-work, market share damage, and bad word-of-mouth.

If we want to look further down the ROI road, take the company that bought that CRM technology. The same losses can be figured for them. They thought that they were buying something that would give them an ROI, but because of re-work and adoption resistance, they also spent their potential profit installing and re-working technology. In addition, what about the resistance of the employees using the system? Their lack of productivity is due to a built-in resistance to change, using a new system, feeling overwhelmed and feeling confused. That lack of productivity costs money! We'll look at the cost of adoption resistance in Section 6.

This may be why technology stock prices have taken such a turn—technology is not being implemented well and the returns for both vendors and buyers isn't there— there is a black hole where all the money is going out. It would be interesting to see these types of calculations added to P&L sheets. The paradigm shift we're trying to create is: "Don't fall into the CRM gap—if you don't do technology implementation well now, you'll pay later."

Market Damage of Poor Service Calculation

There are other aspects to consider when considering what should go onto a balance sheet with respect to customers and their value. In this next section we provide some easy to follow formulas to calculate the market damage due to poor service. In our market damage calculations, we include the following aspects, as well as calculations to balance market damage with the value of the prevention of problems and enhance your customer service:

- impact of negative word of mouth
- impact of poor service
- impact of improving the service
- net value of complaint handling
- prevention of problems

- value of better accessibility of your service

In quantifying the impact of poor service, the primary purpose of this section is to answer the following questions:

- What is the cost of the current level of problems and service?
- What is the return on the investment for improving the service, preventing the problems, and from more responsive complaint handling?

Once you have calculated the value of one customer (see example in figure 9), you can collect more information about your customers to see the value of improving customer service i.e., reduce complaints. You begin by finding out the number of problems or complaints, and with the previously calculated value of the customer, you can follow the steps to see the cost of complaint handling.

Customer Lifetime Value Calculations:

Average Customer Lifetime	=	9
Initial Cost	=	$900
Price of Initial Purchase	=	$5,000
Expected Yearly Additional Revenue	=	$500
Interest Rate	=	9%
Customer Lifetime Value	=	$7,098

Increasing Customer Lifetime Value Calculation:

Price of Initial Purchase of 2nd Product	=	$300
Expected Yearly Additional Revenue	=	$300
Increased Customer Lifetime Value	=	$2,099
Total Customer Lifetime Value	=	$9,196

Market Damage Approximations:

Total Customer Lifetime Value	=	$9,196
Word of Mouth Factor	=	15
Influence Rate	=	100
Lost Profits per Lost Customer	=	$10,576
Number of Complaints	=	100
Percent Complaining	=	11%
# of Customers Experiencing the Problem	=	909
Complaints Resolved Satisfactorily	=	65%
Market Damage	=	$9,984,353

What if...

More people learn of the problem?

Word of Mouth Factor	=	15

More people complain?

Percent Complaining	=	11%

More complaints are resolved satisfactorily?

Complaints Resolved Satisfactorily	=	65%

Customers as Corporate Assets:

Percent of Customers that Score 5	=	14%
Approximate Total Number of Customers	=	100,000
Total Customer Lifetime Value	=	$9,196
Customer Asset	=	$128,747K

Figure 9. Customer lifetime value calculations

Leveraging CRM Analytics to Improve Customer Asset

In this age of product likeness, in which the market fails to perceive any profound difference between products or companies and any product advantage today is copied by the competition tomorrow, quality customer relationship management is the only thing that can place one company head and shoulders above the rest. The mindset for developing a competitive customer service strategy and execution must be different. Knowing that, what if you had data at your fingertips within minutes to know:

1. How your customers feel about your products and/or services?
2. Which products are/are-not doing well?
3. Which products or services are in trouble and why?

And that the improvement initiatives that you are about to undertake will:

1. Win quick management approval because you were able to calculate the ROI

2. Generate ample payoff

3. Produce benefits via a combination of increased revenue and expense reduction

4. Create strategic advantages that help you beat your competition by:

    • maximizing service delivery
    • optimizing productivity
    • increasing market share
    • avoiding unnecessary costs
    • streamlining bureaucracies

That can be the promise of a CRM system if it is leveraged properly. Executives can make their company stand out from the pack by offering such extraordinary service that it makes it hard for customers to look elsewhere. In order to do that, organizations must add an analytical solution to their CRM initiatives. This means executives need to know how to effectively manage the customer lifecycle and understand customer behavior through engagement, transaction, fulfillment and service to insure a business's growth and maximize their customers' lifetime value. Since CRM is a combination of multiple data sources, multiple functions and multiple systems, it can be a complex business process problem to solve.

Measuring All the Elements in a CRM System

In order to fully understand how a customer relationship can become quantifiable, there are three important aspects to consider:

1. Integration of information
2. Analysis of that information
3. Appropriate action to take based on the information

In designing a CRM system that can measure and learn from the data, a company needs the ability to integrate data across all customer touchpoints as customers increasingly embrace multiple e-touchpoints (simple clicks to Web server logs to ad server records and commerce transactions) and as well as to operational CRM systems that feature an increasing number of touchpoints, including: Web, ATM, POS, call center, kiosk, direct sales, mobile devices, etc.

The next step in CRM is to analyze the interaction between the customers and the company touchpoints. This should result in knowledge of which touchpoints have the biggest impact on customer behavior. Then it should be determined what information to gather. An important element in this is Meta data. This is the data that determines the characteristics of the data to be gathered. The collected data is stored in operational databases. These databases are used for the daily operational business processes. From these databases, data is to be selected, extracted and cleaned, to then be stored in a data warehouse. The data warehouse is a data repository that provides extensive multivariate analyses. These multivariate analyses result in the customer knowledge used to increase customer satisfaction and CLV. Analyzing the data for behavioral pattern is done with data mining. This is done with elaborate statistical, logical and mathematical techniques. The last step is when discovered customer knowledge is spread throughout the organization and applied at the various touchpoints to make the products and services better suited to the needs and desires of the customers.

Customer feedback touchpoints can include:

- sales
- marketing and advertising
- inventory management
- quality control
- customer fulfillment
- field services
- customer support contact centers

Measures include:

- customer profitability
- customer segmentation
- customer loyalty

How Increasing CLV Increase Shareholder Value

Taken together, both operational and e-business systems create enormous, granular data sources in "open" formats. They need to be combined, analyzed, measured and augmented with financial data to arrive at such critical indicators as revenue, profitability and ROI. In other words, CRM analysis needs to be intelligent enough and integrative enough to enable customers to measure revenues, profits and customer satisfaction—not just clicks. This integrative type of measuring capacity is what helps organizations to:

- speed decision making
- enhance legacy implementations (i.e., leverage ERP analytics)
- improve margins
- maximize ROI

This integrated information leads to business process mapping and business process re-engineering, which then ties into customer service, CLV and shareholder value. Companies need to analyze more than just the customer service database. They need a tool to bring in the other customer service systems (ACD, IVR, eCare, etc.), the financial, the on- and off-line transactions, the prospecting and affiliating communications. A tool that can enable rich customer analysis needs to be able to:

- measure customer behavior
- strengthen customer loyalty
- quantify customer lifetime value and increase it

A system that can do all that would need to be able to integrate data from all customer touchpoints, and business channels (from operational CRM to front office automation suites) so that the data would be inclusive of product data, financial information, customer demographics as well as psychographic data. In addition, other factors that affect the real measurement are:

- service level agreements
- the interaction center's responsiveness and management of the interaction life cycle

- what is takes to "certify" an interaction center, (which requires deep customer service benchmarking of the services delivered to customers)

Focusing on Analytics

There is a very large difference in analysis versus reporting. While many CRM technologies claim that they provide business analytics, they merely provide simple metrics reporting. That is why many times just purchasing a CRM system needs to be augmented with a system that is specifically designed to process the data from the CRM system.

The trouble with stark data points is they don't provide enough meaningful contexts or rich, textured, and actionable knowledge that can be effectively leveraged by sales, marketing and service channels to measure results and target appropriate changes to key business processes. Without this connection to these other areas the information cannot increase CLV or increase shareholder value and there is little or no return on investment for the CRM system. In fact, it could be a negative expenditure.

Straight reporting is comprised of "dumb" data points that have only a one-time usage. This kind of straight statistical reporting only tells WHAT happened by providing:

- single data sources
- basic top-level data points such as: number of e-mails sent, bounced-back e-mails
- simple counts/segmentation

Intelligent Analytics

In order for the CRM data to give meaning to the bottom-line, another type of reporting is required than the static reporting type. Executives need to have CRM information in an easily digestible form that lends itself to quick decision-making power.

Intelligent CRM analysis is smart, meaningful and manageable information that can be used for repurposing so that it can contribute to the bottom-line. It is analysis that demonstrates what happened, why, when, where and how; providing panoramic customer perspective. Then the next steps/action items are easily identified and leveraged across business channels so that one can change the right things in the business process. Intelligent analysis explains how the TOTAL customer-facing business is functioning, i.e.:

- multiple data sources
- sophisticated reporting
- in-depth, contextualized knowledge

Companies need CRM analysis that drills down to deliver the what, where, why, when and how—the granular—yet contextualized details needed to fully understand the efficiency and effectiveness of today's e-Commerce. The measurements need to go far beyond raw data/metrics reporting by mining, measuring and managing real-time customer interactions/indicators such as Web logs, automatic call distribution systems, and e-commerce transactions to enable business leaders to plan, manage and execute on strategies and processes based on in-depth analyses and understanding of the customer relationship. In addition, a CRM measurement application needs do more than merely run reports that analyze the efficiency of a discrete operation. It needs to illuminate the effectiveness of an entire customer-facing business.

By illuminating the complete business picture, the CRM analytics needs to not only reveal the overall context, but also to reveal critical details like: customer retention and profitability, strategic effectiveness, and workforce optimization.

The solution needs to allow companies to:

- track trends and study historical patterns
- analyze strategies and implementations
- forecast future usage

And then be able to answer questions such as:

- How call volume affects customer service?

- Which products have the greatest impact?

- What aspects of products generate inquiries, and/or positive and negative service levels?

The system would need to show customer retention and profits, strategic effectiveness and workforce optimization. For the data to have real world meaning, it would need to track trends and historical patterns and forecast future usage. An example of the data might be how call volume affects customer service, which products are having the greatest impact in the market place or what aspects of the CRM system are generating good or bad comments—kiosks, e-mail, call center, etc. You might also gain information on how service level agreements are being kept. All of that information, integrated with financial data, can enable companies to measure and keep track of revenue and profitability and determine the ROI of their CRM system.

The development of a management response and control system is enhanced through the collection of easily available process measurements, the selection of which are generally in abundance. More importantly, many of these measurements (which are commonly called "internal metrics") are provided at no extra cost from the standard technologies:

- the PBX, or public phone exchange
- the ACD, or automatic call director
- the IVR, or interactive voice response unit
- the CTI, or computer-telephone integration unit
- the CTS, or contact tracking software
- the RDBMS, or relational database management system
- and many more

Gordon MacPherson of the Incoming Calls Management Institute once defined world-class contact center management as "the art of having the right number of agents in their seats, at the right times, accurately answering a correctly forecasted call load at the appropriate service level and at the lowest possible cost while delighting the majority of callers." Of course, the Herculean challenge is just how to achieve the task as defined above. The goal of this book is to address this challenge in as logical and quantitative a manner as possible.

In Chapter 3, we will focus on:

1. Defining the most popular internal metrics
2. Describing where or how each metric is typically collected or computed
3. Suggesting industry standard goals for each metric
4. Suggesting possible management action if the metric changes

Figure 10 depicts the "big picture" of what we plan to accomplish in this handbook for contact center managers; i.e., a management system that focuses on the telephone call as a critical moment of truth around which a contact center manager must build a custom, reliable, and validated quality of service measurement system. Our management concept simplifies the complexity of a typical contact center into a series of internal and external metrics that must be:

1. Consistently measured, recorded, and tracked

2. Combined and processed into actionable reports

3. Delivered to mission-critical process managers that can take action to improve the telephonic moment of truth for your caller

Figure 10. Measuring the quality of contact center service

Every contact center manager will apply our quality of service measurement system differently, focusing at times on a different set, or more likely on a subset, of internal and external metrics. As discussed, the difference in management style will be driven by the stated mission of the contact center in relation to the strategic direction of the corporation whose customers it serves. However, we have found that regardless of the contact center's tactical mission, the concept diagrammed in figure 10 applies to a holistic process of contact center management.

Contact Center Dynamics

Contact centers are unique environments when compared to virtually any other traditional business unit. Given the important role that contact centers play in achieving the goal of customer satisfaction, it is essential to understand these dynamics in order to provide effective and efficient contact center management.

Perhaps the most unique characteristic of a contact center is the fact that its workload arrives randomly. Customers, not the contact center manager, dictate when work arrives, what type of work is required, and the volume of work to be done. This randomly arriving work load also fluctuates by year, month, day of week, and time of day, making the task of completing work on a timely basis challenging, if not impossible. Consumer reactions to market trends, shifts due to economic and political variances at both the local and international levels will influence contact volume to the center.

Good service, as measured by the time a caller waits to speak with a representative, is dependent upon having the appropriate number of resources available when calls arrive. Any time staff levels fall below caller demand; poor service to callers will result. This fact is particularly important to understand at times when corporate financial results throughout the year suggest that staff reductions are appropriate. When staff is reduced in the contact center, the call volumes continue to arrive resulting in a measurable degradation in service to callers.

The task of maintaining quality customer service and obtaining customer satisfaction has become a measured science. It makes an art of contact center management. Contact center management in itself, is the delicate balance of many tasks and events: workforce management to obtain the optimum in service levels and customer satisfaction, agent training and supervision, quality monitoring and evaluation, and much, much more. The efficient and effective maintenance of this balance is accomplished by setting realistic and measurable goals and management objectives.

A major dynamic influencing contact center management is cost. Unlike virtually any other business unit, a contact center incurs cost the minute it opens its door, regardless of whether or not it provides effective service. Studies prove that when a 1-800 service is provided, poor service is far more costly in hard dollars than good service.

As we will see, service level is only a partial measurement of quality service. Contact volumes and complexity continue to increase (contact volume creep), and more often than not, contact centers are a strategic corporate resource that requires the best of professional management.

Technology Implementation
in percent

Technology	In Place	Planned	Undecided
Interactive Voice Response	56	22	22
Agent Monitoring	39	21	40
Analytic Toolset	31	12	57
Workforce Management	29	18	53
Computer Telephony Integration	23	42	35
Skills-Based Routing	18	10	72
Reader Boards	17	8	75
Customer Interaction Mgmt	7	24	69
Outsourcing Calls	6	15	79
Voice Over Internet Protocol	1	18	81

Figure 11. Sources of contact center data

Sources of Contact Center Data

Automatic Call Directory

- Call frequency
- Caller tolerance for waiting in the queue
- Telephone activity by agent

Integrated Voice Response Unit

- Who is calling the contact center?
- What are they calling about?
- What did they access to get what they wanted?

Voice Network Services

- Who is calling the contact center?
- What are they calling about?
- Did they get through to the contact center?

Data Network Services

- What telecommunications equipment is in use?
- What telecommunications equipment is out of service?
- What software databases are being accessed?

Line Monitoring Devices

- What was discussed?
- How well was it discussed?
- When was it discussed?

Data Terminal Monitoring Devices

- What software was accessed?
- When was it accessed?
- How was it accessed?

Adherence Monitoring Devices

- Which agents are logged on?
- Are they working on telephone calls?
- Are they working as planned?

Computer Assisted Telephone Surveys

- Was the caller satisfied with the call experience?
- Would the caller recommend the contact center to others?
- Did the contact center build loyalty?

Additionally, e-mail and the World Wide Web, commonly referred to as the Internet, also offer additional sources for gaining valuable bits or customer contact data such as:

Electronic Messaging (E-mail)

- E-mail frequency.
- E-mail response time.
- What are they writing about?
- E-mail response per shift.
- E-mail responses per hour.
- Average processing time per response.
- Number of responses per product.
- Peak response times.

Web site interaction

- How many hits does the Web site generate (refer to figure 12)?
- What self-service features are available via Web access?

Possible Choices

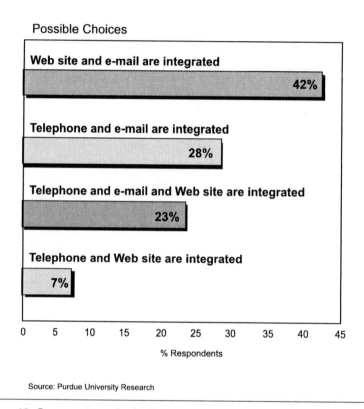

Figure 12. *Integration of telephone, e-mail and Web site*

Contact Center Metrics

Much of this book is devoted to defining contact center metrics and suggesting how to use them. In the remainder of Chapter 3, we will define many of the popular contact center metrics individually, and prescribe some action for you to take if the metric changes. In Chapter 5, we will combine internal and external metrics into a more holistic management decision-making approach.

In addition, in Appendix H, we have grouped the contact center metrics for different measurement purposes. In this appendix you will also find some very interesting and important benchmarking data that can help you compare your contact center metrics against the norm in your industry.

Definition of Metric

 Adherence: This percentage represents how closely an agent adheres to his/her detailed work schedule as provided by the workforce management system. 100% adherence means that the agent was exactly where they were supposed to be at the time projected in their schedule. The scheduled time allows for meetings with the supervisor, education, plus answering customer phone calls.) Adherence is calculated as a percentage equal to (actual time an agent is logged into the system ready to answer the telephone) divided by (the total time the agent is scheduled to be ready to answer the telephone) times 100.

Metric Capture and Reporting

The data for the percent adherence is taken from the ACD and should be reported daily and tracked both weekly and monthly.

Suggested Goal for Metric

Best practices dictate that individual agent adherence should be 92% or better.

Suggested Management Actions

Contact Center Manager

If adherence is below the objective, you might investigate the following:

1. There may be a failure to motivate/educate personnel on the importance of good adherence

2. Supervisory personnel may not be available to coach and support new personnel

3. The agents are potentially misreading the schedule

4. There might be a high absence rate

5. There may be too much mandatory time away from the phone compared to call demand

6. Better use of force management system software

Definition of Metric

After Call Work Time (Wrap-up Time): This is the average amount of time an agent spends on performing follow-up work after an agent has disconnected from the caller.

Metric Capture and Reporting

Wrap-up times by agent, by team, and by contact center are helpful and are available from the ACD. This metric should be tabulated:

- by group
- by individual on a daily, weekly, and monthly basis

Appropriate comparisons to past trends should be made graphically.

Suggested Goal for Metric

The average across industries for wrap-up time is 60 seconds. We suggest a goal range from 30 to 60 seconds.

Suggested Management Actions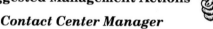

Contact Center Manager

1. When there seems to be a problem with timely wrap-up, and it is not training, process, or technology related, post this metric by group every hour until the situation improves.

2. Supplies to complete the call wrap may not be readily available. Either the distribution or location of them should be changed.

3. Steps over and above what is really needed may have been added to the wrap process. Observe and evaluate all wrap-up activity to determine whether each activity adds value to the process.

4. Encouraging the agent to process information during the actual call can reduce wrap-up time. If you have intuitive and user-friendly software systems in place, this can reduce overall call-handling time and expense, and increase productivity.

5. Excessive call wrap-up indicates an agent problem that needs further study especially via call monitoring to help define the issue.

6. Upward trends in this metric indicate a change in agent behavior. Expect a variance report from the supervisor.

7. Longer wrap-up times on average suggest there are either training, process, or technology issues.

8. If there have been new agents added, then longer wrap-up times due to unfamiliarity could be expected.

9. If the longer times can be traced to certain agents, then re-training is needed.

10. If new layers of bureaucratic data capture have recently been added, then consider whether the additional information is worth the expense.

11. If the issue does not seem to be training or process oriented, then it may mean the technology is due for an upgrade or expansion.

12. Train agents to enter data while talking to customers to reduce wrap-up time to a minimum.

Contact Center Supervisors

1. Wrap-up times are appropriately used in individual and group evaluations of performance. Long wrap-up time impacts queue time, abandonment rates, and can act to decrease caller satisfaction.

2. Increased monitoring can help identify reasons and solutions.

3. The group wrap-up information is particularly helpful if some call types require differing wrap-up activities. In this instance, individual agent wrap-up times should be compared to the group's average. Otherwise individual times can be compared to averages for the contact center as a whole.

Training Manager

1. Training on what steps are necessary to complete the call

2. Telecommunications Manager

3. The screens for completing information are slow and need adjustment or upgrading

Definition of Metric

Average Abandonment Time: This is the average time in seconds a caller waited before abandoning a call. Unless there is a specific industry need, tracking this is not as valuable as tracking the percent abandons.

Metric Capture and Reporting

This is gathered by the ACD and should be reported daily and weekly.

Suggested Goal for Metric

Across industries the average for this metric is 60 seconds. We suggest a target range of 20 to 60 seconds.

Suggested Management Actions

Contact Center Manager

1. Very short abandon times suggest customer impatience either due to the availability of other competitive options or due to disgust from repeated unsuccessful attempts to reach your contact center. Either are cause for concern and action.

2. Check the number of abandoned and blocked calls and the queue times to see whether there is a large problem with callers not getting through. If customers see this as a serious problem, caller satisfaction will fall.

Contact Center Supervisors

1. Add part time agents during the peak call volume times of the day.

Definition of Metric

Average Cost per Call/Contact: This is the sum of all costs for running the contact center for the period divided by the number of calls/contacts received in the contact center for the same period. This would include all calls/contacts for all reasons whether handled by an agent or by technology.

Metric Capture and Reporting

The number of calls received will be captured by the ACD. The total cost of the center can be obtained from your accounting department. This metric should be computed and examined weekly by the contact center management.

Suggested Goal for Metric

This metric varies dramatically by industry. Across industries, our experience shows the metric to average $4 per contact. We suggest adoption of a goal ranging from $2 to $5 per contact.

Suggested Management Actions

Contact Center Manager

1. This is such a high-level metric that nearly every other metric affects it. Drilling down into the component parts will be necessary to determine what needs to be adjusted.

2. Upward trends require close examination of both the number of calls and the fixed and variable costs for the contact center. The likely relationships are as follows:

    - Everything else being equal, the greater the number of calls to the contact center, the higher the costs will be, but the lower the cost per call will be.

    - The greater the percent of VRU handled calls, everything else being equal, the lower the total costs should be. This is because VRU handled calls should be of shorter duration and do not require the intervention and consequent additional costs of an agent.

    - If the number of calls decreases substantially while the fixed contact center costs remain level or increase, the average cost per contact will increase. This suggests that costs could be trimmed. The most likely adjustment should be to staffing:

        o off-peak staffing may need to be decreased

        o part time help may need to be hired for additional on-peak staffing

        o additional training may be needed

    It is also possible that many new agents have been added recently and their lack of experience is translating to longer talk times leading to higher costs. In this case, close supervision to bring new agents along faster will increase costs in the short run, but should pay dividends with shorter talk times.

3. This is a very "visible" area all managers need to track. There should be solid reasons for call costs to fluctuate, which suggest solutions.

4. Contact center cost/FTE (full time equivalent) is an even better measure of contact center efficiency and will be used in later chapters of this handbook.

5. Consider dividing costs into direct and indirect expenses. Remove administrative and variable costs from computation. Calculate 1-800 service cost per contact to justify personnel increase to reduce telephone expense cost and increase customer satisfaction.

Definition of Metric

 Average Handle Time: This is the sum of talk time and after-call work time.

Data Capture and Reporting

The ACD provides the average handle time or AHT. It should be run daily and investigated weekly and monthly. You can design an AHT report formatted by employee, by team, and by contact center. A trend line graph will be generated.

Suggested Goal for Metric

The average handle time goal would depend on contact center type. For a technical support contact center on typical items such as VCRs, home office equipment, etc., averages are between 10 and 15 minutes.

Across industries, the average handle time is 8.5 minutes. We suggest targeting this metric between 3 and 10 minutes ±15%. A hoped for trend here is flat to decreasing. It is probably best if you can develop a range based on call types and shifts. By creating a range that is acceptable you avoid the single number target issue and give agents the option to take as long as necessary to handle the call completely the first time.

Suggested Management Actions

Contact Center Manager

1. Track a trend line and make this graph a center-wide, visible item

2. Ask the front-line supervisor to report on variances outside of the target range

3. Long AHT can indicate overstaffing, which will lead to higher costs

4. Agent training is required either in technical product details, or telephone handling skills

Contact Center Supervisors

1. Too few (or too many) agents were scheduled
2. Scripting for the contact center agents may be inadequate/inaccurate
3. Adherence to scheduled time is low
4. By talking with agents and monitoring calls, investigate and explain variance outside of targeted goals

Human Resources Manager

1. Be aware of trends and recruiting standards

Training Manager

1. Add training to tactfully end calls when the transaction is complete
2. Better training on specific services or products
3. Better training to access information in computer databases
4. Work with supervisors to identify remedial training needs
5. Employees can listen to each other's calls to discover ways (best practices) to maintain the targeted range

Information Technology Manager

1. Ensure that technology is delivering accurate/timely information

Telecommunications Manager

1. Ensure that the switch technology is not creating transfer issues

Other Departments

1. Internal department-to-department communications may have failed. For example, if Marketing is running a new promotional program, the contact center may not readily know how to respond to customer questions. The same can be said for new products and services of which the center is unaware.

Definition of Metric

 Average Hold Time: This is the average number of seconds that an agent places customers on hold.

Metric Capture and Reporting

The ACD can report the hold time by agent and give an average number of seconds. Report and plot this metric daily, weekly, and monthly and do a management review weekly and monthly.

Suggested Goal for Metric

Across industries hold time averages 60 seconds. We suggest targeting hold times between 20 and 60 seconds.

Suggested Management Actions

Contact Center Manager

Excessive hold time usually means agents don't have ready access to critical information or the freedom to create solutions for callers. Any of the following could be true:

1. Lack of information at the disposal of the agent.
2. Training needs because agents do not know how to get to the necessary information.
3. System glitches, which means that it takes too long for information to come up.
4. Lack of empowerment at the front line.
5. This is a critical metric for contact center managers to watch. Hold time directly impacts caller dissatisfaction.
6. This metric is difficult to use, as agents prefer to use the mute button on a headset rather than hold.

Contact Center Supervisors

1. An upward trend in hold time indicates a change in agent behavior or caller demands.
2. Selectively monitor agents to investigate increases in hold time.

Training Manager

1. Long hold times or an increase in hold time for an individual agent can indicate the need for additional training on where to find answers quickly.
2. Guard against agents using hold time for the benefit of avoiding "dead air" time with the caller. Training can be given on how to handle the "dead air" time, which can create a more confident agent.

3. Hold times will be longer and more frequent for agents who cannot type well while talking to callers. This problem should be identified before new agents matriculate out of basic telephone training.

4. Agents should use hold time only when absolutely necessary and with the permission of the caller. You can use the analogy of face-to-face service and say you would never just walk away from a customer without excusing yourself.

Information Technology Manager

1. The pop screens or other means by which agents get information may not be working properly.

Telecommunications Manager

1. Researching causes for long hold time. This can help the company discover communication problems and information flow barriers.

Other Departments

1. The information needed by the agent may not be in the system for the agent to access during the call. New products, services, or programs may have been instituted without due preparation and contact center involvement.

Definition of Metric

 Average Number of Rings: This is the average number of rings the customer hears before the call is answered by the system whether by an agent, an IVRU, or a VRU.

Metric Capture and Reporting

This data is gathered by the ACD. Reporting should be daily for contact center management and as needed for the caller satisfaction program.

Suggested Goal for Metric

Across industries, the average number of rings is 2 or 3. We suggest targeting the number of rings between 2 to 4.

Suggested Management Actions

Contact Center Manager

1. The average number of rings needs to be kept to a minimum, though at peaks it may vary. Thus average number of rings should be discussed. Also, number of rings can be set as a parameter at the switch as a tool to manage queue time.

2. This is not significant for caller satisfaction as long as they don't receive a busy signal.

Contact Center Supervisors

1. If agents manually answer their telephones, ensure they know the standard.

Training Manager

1. Make agents aware of the contact center goal.

Definition of Metric

 Average Queue Time: This is the average number of seconds the caller spends waiting for an agent to answer the telephone after being placed in the queue by the ACD.

Metric Capture and Reporting

The ACD can give this data by application or call type for all calls for the center. It can be posted daily, weekly, and monthly for all contact center employees to see.

Suggested Goal for Metric

This is an industry specific metric. Across industries the queue time averages 150 seconds. We suggest targeting queue times to between 30 seconds and 90 seconds. Queue time is a critical factor in establishing your overall service level targets. Having zero queue time would indicate that you are spending money to have agents waiting for calls to arrive and this would be inefficient and costly.

Suggested Management Actions

Contact Center Manager

1. There may be new methods for the agents to manage, or a change in policy that requires more handle time.

2. There may be too many inexperienced agents scheduled.

3. You might add IVR for more routine call handling.

4. You might try using CTI to mechanize some agent work tasks.

5. Many contact centers use visible LED display boards to communicate average queue time and the number of callers holding in queue. This is typically broadcast on a real-time basis.

6. Queue time can be a major sunk cost of a contact center.

7. Queue time is also a major driver of caller dissatisfaction.

8. Consider adding part-time agents during peak call volumes.

9. Staffing by demand will allow you to consistently meet these service goals.

10. If you are using 1-800 service, it pays to keep queue times low.

Contact Center Supervisors

1. Report queue time by call type where agents can see the problem. Doing so creates a potential for partnership in resolving the issues that are creating the increased queue time

2. agents that are being utilized in other splits and/or with other work such as fulfillment, letter responses, survey analysis, and Internet responses could be pulled to reduce queue time.

3. Spend time in the beginning with all agents to ensure they understand the impact queue time has on the other metrics like abandonment, caller satisfaction, and telephone costs.

4. Also spend time to demonstrate how adherence to schedules, hold time, average handle time, and absenteeism can impact queue time. Schedule adherence is a big factor in performing well on this metric. Agents leaving early or returning late from breaks, lunch, meetings, or training can cause major queue time problems and are therefore a major set of opportunities for improvement. For example, a team of 12 people taking an extra 5 minutes to get back from a team meeting each week can create 52 hours of lost time to the contact center each year.

5. By publishing queue time on the bulletin board, agents who know there are long queues in certain applications or call types may take the lead in resolving the issue.

6. Typically agents can help lengthy queue times by speeding up their answers.

Human Resources Manager

1. Consider linking group agent performance and group compensation/bonuses to keep queue time to a minimum.

Training Manager

1. During initial training, spend time with all agents to ensure they understand what the impact queue time has on the other metrics like caller abandons, caller satisfaction, and costs.

2. During initial training, spend time to demonstrate how adherence to schedules, hold time, average handle time, and absenteeism can impact queue time.

Telecommunications Manager

1. Calls can become hung up in the ACD and this is a technical issue that needs the attention of the telecommunications staff. A hung call can actually remain there for hours if not detected, and this can impact your average queue time.

2. Use the VRU to offer caller self-help, or other methods of leaving number for call backs to reduce queue time.

3. Tell the caller how many people are ahead in the queue.

4. Estimate for the caller how many seconds or minutes they will most likely have to wait to talk to an agent.

5. Encourage callers to call back during a less busy time, and tell the caller when that time would most likely be based on call volume records.

Definition of Metric

 Average Speed of Answer: This is the total queue time, divided by the number of calls handled. This includes both IVR-handled calls as well as calls handled by a live agent.

Data Capture and Reporting

This metric is available directly from the ACD and should be reported in half hour increments and plotted for trend detection.

Suggested Goal for Metric

This metric, commonly referred to as the ASA, is frequently targeted to be less than 20 seconds.

Suggested Management Actions

Contact Center Manager

If the average speed of answer is too high, it may indicate:

1. Wrap-up time has extended beyond established objective
2. Higher than expected holding time
3. Poor forecast of call volumes
4. Poor adherence to schedules by agents

Definition of Metric

 Average Talk Time: This represents the total number of seconds the caller was connected to an agent.

Metric Capture and Reporting

Talk time is gathered and reported by the ACD by agent, by group, or by contact center and should be assessed weekly and monthly. If specific types of calls they handle group agents, the metric can be even more helpful as a management tool. Individual versus group performance can be a powerful feedback tool, but it is important to balance this with feedback from the caller satisfaction program by agent. If somewhat longer talk times lead to higher ratings of satisfaction, then the extra cost may be justified. It may be that other agents need additional training on interpersonal skills to increase customer satisfaction by use of slightly longer talk times.

Suggested Goal for Metric

Across industries, talk time averages 330 seconds. For technical support calls, this can be 6 to 10 minutes. We suggest targeting talk time between 270 and 360 seconds.

Suggested Management Actions

Contact Center Manager

1. Talk time variance indicates change in either agent or caller behavior. Expect your supervisors to be able to identify reasons and assist with solutions.

2. By asking the caller after the call to answer several satisfaction and expectation questions, average talk time can be honed to a desirable length.

3. Talk time also can vary depending on the skills of the agent, availability of information to the agent, or systems issues.

4. It is more meaningful to examine talk time with reference to a given type of call.

5. In general, in order to keep costs low, short talk times are desirable. However, short talk times can lead to dissatisfaction among callers who feel they were not listened to or were rushed.

6. Talk times vary by agent style of communication. This is difficult to manage or change. Extremely short or long talk time (against group averages) should be investigated.

Contact Center Supervisors

1. Increased monitoring will help identify what is causing trends.

Training Manager

1. Training on how to end calls
2. Training on keyboarding while talking
3. Training on how to find information quickly

Telecommunications Manager

1. If there are problems with the technology that brings information to the agents, then talk times could be longer than necessary.

Other Departments

1. New services, products, or programs instituted without contact center training could increase talk times.

Definition of Metric

 Calls per Hour: This is simply the average number of calls that an agent handles per hour, and is equal to the total calls handled during one working shift divided by the total time logged into the telephone system.

Data Capture and Reporting

The data to calculate calls per hour is available from the ACD, and should be reported daily by agent.

Suggested Goal for Metric

The calls per hour metric depends substantially upon the nature of the contact center. In a highly technical contact center, this number may be as low as 5 calls per hour, while in a simple inquiry contact center, this metric could be as high as 100 calls per hour.

Suggested Management Actions

Contact Center Manager

Traditionally, calls per hour have been an almost universal measure of agent performance. Agents with many calls per hour were thought to be highly desirable and very productive. As the contact center evolved, this metric has become more suspect and problematic because:

1. A calls-per-hour focus can be a source of lower-quality calls.

2. Agents can figure out ways to trick the system into increasing their calls per hour.

3. With a varying call volume and skill-based routing, the agent does not always have control of calls per hour when not enough calls are received.

Definition of Metric

 Monitoring Scores: These are the results of qualitative grading of agent calls by quality assurance specialists.

Data Capture and Reporting

Monitoring scores do not have one common measurement system, although they are normally graded on a one hundred-point scale. It is recommended that agents be monitored four to five times per month for compliance to policy and for contact center standard responses.

Suggested Goal for Metric

A general goal is not applicable for this metric.

Suggested Management Actions

Contact Center Manager

1. Scores should be consistently generated.

2. Agents should be thoroughly familiar with the scoring methods.

3. If possible, the monitored call should be taped so that actual grading can be compared with the agent listening to the recorded call.

Definition of Metric

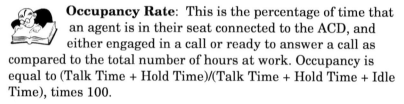 **Occupancy Rate**: This is the percentage of time that an agent is in their seat connected to the ACD, and either engaged in a call or ready to answer a call as compared to the total number of hours at work. Occupancy is equal to (Talk Time + Hold Time)/(Talk Time + Hold Time + Idle Time), times 100.

Data Capture and Reporting

The metrics to make this calculation are available from the ACD. Reporting should be averaged by agent by working shift.

Suggested Goal for Metric

A common goal for this metric is a best practice of 90% or greater.

Suggested Management Actions

Contact Center Manager

1. Suggest better agent training
2. Suggest better agent supervision

Definition of Metric

 Percent Abandon: This is the percentage of calls that get connected to the ACD, but get disconnected by the caller before reaching an agent, or before completing a process within the IVR. The abandon rate is the percent of calls that are abandoned compared to all calls received.

Metric Capture and Reporting

The ACD can report this metric for the contact center and the report should be run daily, weekly, and monthly. You must define the length of "short abandon" calls and ensure that you eliminate them from your data collection and reporting. "Short abandon" is usually defined as 20 seconds or less.

Suggested Goal for Metric

Across industries, the abandon rate is 3%. We suggest targeting an abandon rate of between 3 to 5%. Abandonment is almost completely dependent upon the caller and may vary due to any one or all of the following:

1. Caller motivation related to the degree of urgency
2. Availability of other contact centers that may be called for the answer
3. Caller expectation based upon demographics
4. Caller available time to wait
5. Cost of the call, i.e., 1-800 versus 1-900 number call

Suggested Management Actions

Contact Center Manager

1. Average waiting time may be too long.
2. Forecast is probably too low.
3. There is increased holding time due to work content change or customer dissatisfaction issues.
4. The holding queue is unacceptable.
5. You might consider using IVR with CTI application to handle some of the more routine calls.
6. You might consider using an overflow group, i.e., outsource some calls.
7. Several times a day you can post the abandon rate for all agents to see. This can be accompanied by some summary explanation of why you may be seeing an increase or decrease in abandoned calls.
8. Calls may be taking longer (increased average handle time), and thus, the staffing level could be insufficient to handle the call traffic.
9. Over time you may see a change in the call arrival pattern, and thus a change in call volumes.
10. Large abandon rates indicate that the queue time is too long. There are ACD reports that show call duration before abandon. If many callers are hanging up within 1 to 5

seconds, there may be a problem with misdirected calls—not a queue problem.

11. Abandoned calls are an indicator of staffing not aligned with volume.

12. Looking at call length, average delay in queue, and schedule adherence can help identify if additional staffing is required.

13. Abandon calls go hand in hand with wait time (queue time). Your customers' tolerance to hold will vary based on their need for the service provided or alternatives available.

Contact Center Supervisors

1. If agent adherence to assigned schedules is not being maintained, your staff is not in place to handle the volume.

2. Non-adherence can be caused by agents not being signed on and available (gossiping), or it could be non-attendance due to something like a flu epidemic.

Human Resources Manager

1. Calls are taking longer (increasing average handle time), and thus, the staffing level is insufficient to handle the traffic.

Telecommunications Manager

1. Failure in the service delivery system can spike volume.

Other Departments

Volume increases due to advertising or some unplanned event such as a technological failure in the service delivery system can cause a spike in call volume.

Definition of Metric

Percent Agent Utilization: Agent utilization is the percentage of time that an agent is in their seat ready to handle calls as compared to the actual time they are in telephone mode. Utilization equals the product of average call handle time (talk time + hold time + after call work time) and the average number of inbound calls per agent per 8-hour shift (ACPS), divided by total time the agent is connected to the ACD and ready to handle calls during a shift, i.e., occupancy (not in percent). This metric is calculated by:

$$Utilization = \frac{(ATT + ACW)(ACPS)}{Occupancy} X100$$

Data Capture and Reporting

The metrics for this calculation are available from the ACD.

Suggested Goal for Metric

The suggested best practice value of this metric is 90% or better.

Suggested Management Actions

Contact Center Manager

1. This metric gives you visibility on the number of agents handling calls as a percentage of the number of agents logged in the system.

2. If low, agents are involved in tasks other than call handling.

Definition of Metric

 Percent Attendance: This is a percentage representing how often an agent is NOT absent from work due to an unplanned absence (not to include excused absences, i.e., vacation, FMLA, jury duty, etc.). Take the total number of unexcused absences and divide it by the total number of days that the agent was expected to be at work, and subtract that number from 100.

Data Capture and Reporting

Automated personnel attendance forms are the most typical method of capturing this data.

Suggested Goal for Metric

This metric will vary considerably, but a goal often seen is 95%.

Suggested Management Actions

Contact Center Manager

If the percent attendance is low, you might:

1. Check for motivational issues

2. Interview the agent to better understand personal problems encountered

Definition of Metric

 Percent Blocked Calls: These are calls that never make it to your ACD. Examples of blocked calls are: busy signals, number not in service messages, etc. This

number can be provided only by your telecommunications provider.

Metric Capture and Reporting

This data is gathered by the ACD or by your telephone service provider and should be examined hourly to see where the peaks in calls occur.

Suggested Goal for Metric

Across industries, 1% of all calls are blocked. We suggest targeting the blocked calls rate to between 1 and 3%. Ideally there should never be any blocked calls since they either mean lost business or an already irritated customer has yet another complaint to add to the list. Neither can be good for the company no matter whether the focus is immediate revenues or long-term caller satisfaction.

Suggested Management Actions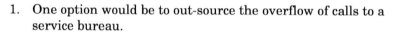

Contact Center Manager

1. One option would be to out-source the overflow of calls to a service bureau.

2. If that is already being done and the abandon rate is also high, it may be the company with which the out-sourced contact was made needs to increase staffing.

3. Increase current staffing with either full or part time agents.

4. Provide more training if queue, talk, hold, etc., times have increased.

5. Blocked calls require customers to redial. If blockage is high, redial rates go up. If a manager looks at call attempts and figures this represents the number of customers, then large errors can result.

6. Most telephone service providers (AT&T, Sprint, MCI) have real time reports that use automatic number identification over a time frame (say 30 days) to identify specific numbers of redials by time of day and day of the week. This information helps in forecasting agent availability.

7. Many carriers can provide statistical packages that normalize busies by removing multiple attempts by originating phone numbers. Suggest surveying customers that have been blocked to quantify loss to business.

8. Busies result in returned products in the retail environment.

Contact Center Supervisors

1. Some telephone service providers allow for the setting of a busy trunk signal when it is not desirable to have callers leave a number for a return call.

2. Use of a busy signal could be justified when the messaging disk is nearly full, or because the number of return calls requested given the number of agents has already been reached.

Human Resources Manager

1. Increase current staffing with either full or part time help.

Telecommunications Manager

1. Technology linking the two centers may not be working properly and, therefore, the customer experiences an additional delay.

Definition of Metric

 Percent Calls Handled on the First Call: This is the percentage of calls that do not require an additional call to the contact center, or return calls by the agent in order to resolve the issue in the original call.

Data Capture and Reporting

The ACD can provide this information in coding during the wrap-up of the call. This needs to be reported daily by agent and by the contact center.

Suggested Goal for Metric

The average for this metric across industries is 85%. We suggest that you target a range between 85 and 100%. This metric is very sensitive to caller satisfaction; i.e., callers greatly value having their questions answered and their problems resolved in the first call.

Suggested Management Actions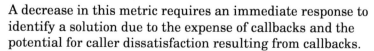

Contact Center Manager

A decrease in this metric requires an immediate response to identify a solution due to the expense of callbacks and the potential for caller dissatisfaction resulting from callbacks.

1. Agent needs to be empowered to make decisions on caller requests that used to require a call back.

2. If there is little blockage and low abandon rates, redial information is helpful to spot splits or areas that may need investigation to ascertain why callers are prone to call back more frequently.

3. Training may be useful. Availability of information to agents should be investigated.

4. Getting the agent involved with solutions is important.

Definition of Metric

 Percent of Calls Placed in Queue: This metric is simply the number of calls placed in the queue, divided by the total of all calls received by the center.

Metric Capture and Reporting

The data for this metric is gathered by the ACD. It should be computed and examined weekly by the contact center manager.

Suggested Goal for Metric

Across industries, 15% of calls are placed in the queue. We suggest a target range from 10 to 20%.

Suggested Management Actions

Contact Center Manager

1. You might investigate an increase in the number of agents— whether full time, part time, or outsourced.

2. Knowing that an increase in this metric can cause an increase in telephone costs, investigating the root causes can be an important item.

Definition of Metric

 Percent of Calls Transferred: This is the percent of total calls transferred from the original agent to someone else.

Metric Capture and Reporting

The ADC can report this metric by agent, and it should be reported daily, weekly, and monthly with agents given feedback at least monthly, preferably weekly. You will want to define what constitutes a transferred call.

Suggested Goal for Metric

Across industries, the average for this metric is 3%. We suggest only one transfer per 100 calls, and always make that transfer to someone with the expertise or authority to handle the call.

Suggested Management Actions

Contact Center Manager

1. If agents have differing skills, then a skills-based routing software should be in use, which will match caller needs to agent abilities.

2. If an agent must transfer a call, time and money can be saved by automatically transferring the caller's record as well.

3. Blind transfers usually mean the caller must explain the situation again, and this repetition negatively impacts caller satisfaction.

4. Define at the outset whether transfers will be announced or blind and try not to stray from this decision. Changing this process back and forth will create undue confusion in the agents.

5. Some companies use blind transfers only during busy times, but agents may not always remember which process is currently in use.

6. Having large quantities of transferred calls indicates a problem. Customers are confused as to either what 1-800 number to call, other 1-800 numbers are blocked, or agents lack necessary information.

7. Transferring large quantities of calls costs money. Careful studies, which include agent and caller focus groups, should be established to identify and correct this problem.

8. Ask for variance reporting from the supervisors along with potential solutions to reduce transfers.

Contact Center Supervisors

1. Attention to this metric should be at the individual agent level. Regular and on-going discussions should occur. In the discussion you can discover training needs and issues with information flow to your agents.

2. Positive recognition for employees who have low transfer rates can create an environment of continuous learning for all agents.

3. High transfer rates can indicate a lack of confidence in their ability to answer caller questions or a lack of needed training.

4. Guard against agents who transfer everything, and seem to have high numbers of calls handled, but are really not serving the caller at the initial point of contact. This can cause morale problems with those taking the transfers. Agents look to management to catch this and stop it.

5. Silent monitoring can be a way of discovering if people are transferring calls that they should be able to handle. Rarely will agents step forward and say they can't handle a call type.

6. Increases in this metric require increased monitoring to identify why calls are being transferred.

Training Manager

1. Make sure that a caller is only transferred once and to someone who can resolve the issue.

2. Increases in transfers within a contact center can indicate that the center is fielding calls of a type the staff is not trained to handle.

Definition of Metric

 Percent Offered Calls Answered: This metric is equal to calls answered, divided by calls offered, times 100.

Data Capture and Reporting

The data for calculating this metric is available from the ACD. A daily report is recommended.

Suggested Goal for Metric

The typical goal for this metric is 98%.

Suggested Management Actions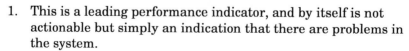

Contact Center Manager

1. This is a leading performance indicator, and by itself is not actionable but simply an indication that there are problems in the system.

2. Scan trends of all other metrics for clues used for problem resolution alternatives.

3. There may be a temporary peak in offered calls.

4. Open line requirements may be too low.

5. Forecast call volume may be too low.

6. There may be too many inexperienced agents scheduled.

7. The intra-flow of vectoring may be inadequate.

8. You might consider IVR with CTI application to handle some of the more routine calls.

9. You might consider using outsourcing for overflow calls.

10. There may be improper use of historical trends in forecasting.

11. There might be poor marketing projection on new promotion/sales announcements.

12. There may be seasonal trends missed or off-schedule.

13. There may be poor adherence to schedules by agents.

Definition of Metric

 Service Level: The formula for service level is calls answered in less than X seconds, divided by offered calls, times 100.

Data Capture and Reporting

The data to calculate service levels is readily available from the ACD. Service levels should be monitored on a continuous basis since this is a leading indicator of problems.

Suggested Goal for Metric

The most popular goal throughout industries is 80% of the calls answered in 20 seconds.

Suggested Management Actions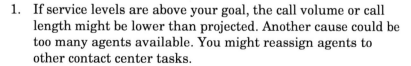

Contact Center Manager

1. If service levels are above your goal, the call volume or call length might be lower than projected. Another cause could be too many agents available. You might reassign agents to other contact center tasks.

2. If service levels are lower than your goal, use other metrics to identify the probable cause of the problem.

3. Possible areas to review for problems are:

- poor forecast of call volumes

- poor adherence to schedules by agents

- poor work prioritization by supervisors

- inadequate review of historical data and other diagnostic data indicators

- schedules may need a review of lunch/breaks start times and end times

Definition of Metric

 Total Calls Offered: This metric represents all calls presented to the contact center including blocked, abandoned, and handled.

Data Capture and Reporting

This metric is captured by the ACD or by the telephone line provider and should be examined hourly, daily, weekly, and monthly. It is necessary to track the calls coming in and break down the results in small units for staffing purposes. Early warning of changes in call patterns allow management to adjust quickly and efficiently.

Suggested Goal for Metric

This metric is primarily used to determine other metrics and to plan and forecast calls and do workforce management.

Suggested Management Actions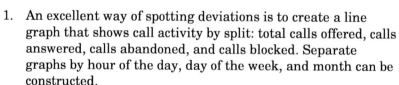

Contact Center Manager

1. An excellent way of spotting deviations is to create a line graph that shows call activity by split: total calls offered, calls answered, calls abandoned, and calls blocked. Separate graphs by hour of the day, day of the week, and month can be constructed.

2. Assess this data by call types so you can determine if callers are making multiple attempts and increasing the number of calls.

3. If the calls offered are changing substantially from the past or from what is expected, it will be necessary to seek an explanation, but one will not be available from looking at ACD generated metrics. The answer will probably be found outside the contact center system. For example, calls offered may increase dramatically due to new programs or promotions offered by your firm or due to the collapse of a former competitor in your field.

4. Total calls offered must be looked at in conjunction with busy data. If under-trunked, calls offered will be limited.

Contact Center Supervisors

1. Increased monitoring will help the supervisor discover the reasons for variance. If there is an increase, attempt to see if there is an increase in repeat callers.

Other Departments

1. Marketing promotions, new product or service introductions, etc., could account for call volume increases. Competitive actions in any of these areas could account for decreases in calls offered. The decision of a competitor may cause calls to increase and this suggests an opportunity for Marketing to capture additional market share.

Definition of Metric

 Agent Turnover: This is the number of agents who left in the course of the period (month, quarter, or year) as a percentage of the total number of full time agents working during that same period.

Data Capture and Reporting

This metric usually is produced by the Human Resources department. It needs to be examined monthly and quarterly.

Suggested Goal for Metric

Across industries, the average for turnover is 25%. We suggest targeting this metric between 15 and 30%.

Suggested Management Actions

Contact Center Manager

1. Always have an exit interview with agents by a non-contact center Human Resources professional. Useful and actionable

information may result, and corrective actions taken, before more valuable agents follow.

2. We have found that compensation is one of the least frequent reasons why agents leave. Usually there are supervision issues, work environment, and/or too much performance pressure such that the environment is experienced as a "sweat shop" by the agents.

3. Knowing the reasons for increased turnover is a constant contact center manager challenge.

4. The average industry cost to recruit, screen, train, and prepare a new agent is approximately $7,000. Agent turnover is one of the major costs of contact centers.

5. Some turnover is good! Low turnover could mean agents are not accountable or not challenged enough to continuously improve.

Contact Center Supervisors

1. In-depth review of exit interview results will help to pinpoint solutions to correct an increase in turnover.

Human Resources Manager

1. Gathering and reviewing accurate exit interview information is critical.

Definition of Metric

 New Hire Training Hours: This is the average amount of time necessary, to train agents in order for them to become fully self-sufficient.

Metric Capture and Reporting

The data for this metric is gathered by Human Resources.

Suggested Goal for Metric

This should be on par with industry or peer group averages.

Suggested Management Actions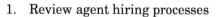

Contact Center Manager

1. Review agent hiring processes

2. Review training curriculum and qualifications of trainers

3. Develop a feedback system among training, call quality monitoring, and supervisors

4. Determine best profile (education, training, skills, etc.) for the job description

Definition of Metric

 Cost to Bring on a New Agent: This metric represents the average cost of training an agent, which includes the following: advertisement fees, recruiting costs, drug testing costs, aptitude testing costs, the trainee's salary for the training period, the trainer's salary for the training time (divided by the number of trainees in the class), the mentor's salary (if applicable), etc. Include any cost directly associated with hiring and training a new agent on board.

Metric Capture and Reporting

The data for this metric is gathered by Human Resources and the Training department.

Suggested Goal for Metric

This should be on par with the average for your industry or peer group.

Suggested Management Actions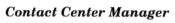

Contact Center Manager

1. Review agent hiring processes

2. Investigate advantages of in-sourcing/outsourcing

3. Review recruiting strategies

4. Review retention strategies

Contact Center Supervisors

1. If agents have differing skills, then a skills-based routing software should be in use, which will match caller needs to agent abilities

Definition of Metric

 Percent handled by caller self-service: This metric measures what percentage of customers are able to obtain the help or service they seek without agent intervention.

Data Capture and Reporting

The data for calculating this metric is available from the ACD and IVR/VRU. A daily report is recommended.

Suggested Goal for Metric

The recommended goal for this metric is greater than 10%.

Suggested Management Actions

Contact Center Manager

1. Review channels of self-service and options available to callers

2. Review and optimize IVR/VRU menu trees and scripts

3. Review on-hold messages

4. Review call-quality monitoring

5. Review call center performance reporting

6. Review customer satisfaction measurement processes

Definition of Metric

Average Entry Error Rate: This represents how many errors per 1,000 calls were generated by your agents. An error is a mistake that costs your company time and/or money to correct/resolve.

Data Capture and Reporting

Use incident tracking through a CRM process to capture this metric. This metric should be reported and followed by all levels of operations management via daily management reports.

Suggested Goal for Metric

The sought after goal across all industries is to maintain an average entry error rate of less than 2%.

Suggested Management Actions

Contact Center Manager

1. Use quality monitoring enabled with screen-scrape technology to determine introduction point of error.

Contact Center Supervisors

1. Conduct side-by-side in-cube coaching and mentoring

2. Schedule retraining for recurring issues

Training Manager

1. Prepare training syllabus and conduct training for recurring issues

Definition of Metric

 Top Box C-sat: This metric represents the percentage of your callers that gave you a perfect score on the question, "Overall, how satisfied were you with the service you received during your call to our company?" (A "perfect" score of 5 out of 5, 7 out of 7, or the top of whatever scale you use). In other words, on whatever scale used, what percentage of your customers selected the top number to reflect that they could not be more satisfied (i.e., "extremely satisfied" or "very satisfied"—the highest score possible)?

Data Capture and Reporting

To capture and report this metric, you must first have a customer satisfaction survey measurement mechanism in place. The result of surveys should be reported on a frequent and regular basis to all operations management levels.

Suggested Goal for Metric

This best practice goal for this metric is 65% or better across all industries.

Suggested Management Actions

Contact Center Manager

1. Develop a caller feedback strategy that captures the voice of the customer with respect to how they feel their calls were handled.

2. Use this feedback process to generate positive customer-interactions and develop best practices behaviors within your contact center.

Definition of Metric

 Bottom Box C-sat: This metric is the converse of Top Box C-sat, and is the percentage of your callers that gave you the lowest score on the question, "Overall, how satisfied were you with the service you received during your call to our company?" (The "lowest" score of 1 out of 5, 7 out of 7, or the bottom of whatever scale you use). Simply speaking, what percentage of your customers selected the option to reflect that they could not be more dissatisfied (i.e., "extremely dissatisfied" or "very dissatisfied"—the lowest score possible) on whatever scale you used?

Data Capture and Reporting

To capture and report this metric, you must first have a customer satisfaction survey measurement mechanism in place. The result of surveys should be reported on a frequent and regular basis to all operations management levels.

Suggested Goal for Metric

This best practice goal for this metric is less than 3% across all industries.

Suggested Management Actions

Contact Center Manager

1. Develop a caller feedback strategy that captures the voice of the customer with respect to how they feel their calls were handled

2. Use this feedback process to generate positive customer-interactions and develop best practices behaviors within your contact center

CHAPTER 4: EXTERNAL METRICS—MEASURING THE HEARTBEAT OF THE CUSTOMER

Introduction

As we discussed in Chapter 1, the primary mission of customer service is to engineer each call in such a way as to delight the caller. Delight results in an increasing probability of customer retention, hence increasing the customer lifetime value and willingness to recommend your product or service to others.

As we discussed in Chapter 2, your customers experience a *'Moment Of Truth'* (MOT) every time they call your contact center for assistance. In figure 10, we diagrammed the measurement of the telephonic MOT by determining internal and external metrics, which can be used as online feedback to those specific process managers that support the contact center and impact this critical MOT for your callers.

An MOT is any and every event where a customer might experience and access the performance of your product or service. An MOT is both a data gathering and a decision-generating event. The customer metaphorically stands at the crossroads and decides to reuse or recommend your contact center to others or vows to never use the contact center service again.

Of course, the real threat is not a decision never to use the contact center again, but rather a decision to discontinue use of the core service/product of the company. Such a decision would lead inevitably to replacement by a competitor's offering. This fact further strengthens our CLV/financial argument of Chapter 2. In other words, the contact center is creating value for the firm that can be quantified and claimed by the manager.

The findings from our research (Monger, 1996) suggest that measuring the caller's perception of the call is best done immediately after the call has been completed rather than hours, days, or weeks later. In this way, it is most possible to capture the caller's actual experience at the MOT.

We have found that a comprehensive, well-designed, and well-executed caller satisfaction (CS) measurement program can generate reliable external metrics which can be driven into internal business process metrics as shown in figure 13.

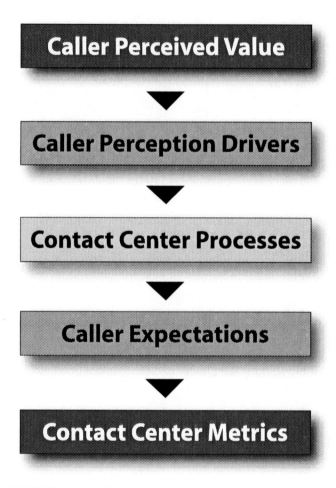

Figure 13. Connecting external metrics to internal metrics

A CS measurement program can also ensure that quality improvement initiatives are properly focused on issues that are most important to the caller. The direct objective of a CS measurement program is to generate valid and consistent caller feedback; i.e., to quantify the perception of the caller which can then be used to initiate positive service strategies.

In trying to better understand what is going to be measured and how the results relate to loyalty and repurchase, we have found it important to approximate the mind-set of customers. Recall from figure 5 that in general, the customer's mind-set will fall in one of three measurable categories:

- Rejection—Very likely to take business elsewhere.
- Acceptance—Service is adequate, but given another alternative customer will probably leave.
- Preference—These are the loyal customers you must strive to retain! When given a choice, you will be selected more often.

An important theme of the external metrics (CS) measurement is to identify attributes for improvement that will increase your ability to move customers from the acceptance category to the preference category. As we will see later, customers who prefer you are actually a quantifiable asset to the company.

Seeing the CS measurement program as an integral part of continuous quality improvement is crucial to demonstrating the return on investment (ROI) of the contact center as follows:

1. Through selecting the process or processes for change that will maximize the impact on customer satisfaction and loyalty
2. By preventing erosion of the customer base
3. By increasing the occurrence of recommendations
4. By minimizing negative word-of-mouth
5. By better understanding what the customer perceives to be value-added

We need to clearly contrast the internal metrics, which were discussed in Chapter 3, from the external metrics, which are the focus of this chapter. Internal metrics are generated by computers internal to your PBX, ACD, or VRU or through departments such as Human Resources and Accounting. They are "hard" numbers that deal with precise reality. For instance, the average queue time today was 6 minutes and 42 seconds. There were .6 transfers per call. The abandon rate was 3%. Agent turnover was 22% last year. The average cost per call last year was $5.67.

External metrics do not have the exactness that can be attributed to a computer or an accounting system, but instead are the "soft" numbers of caller perception that express opinions or emotions which means qualitative measures. Average queue time may have been 6 minutes and 42 seconds, but the customer may perceive it as 15 minutes and way too long. This is the reality the customer will use in decision making for repurchase, recommendation, and continued loyalty. Therefore, we should apply the axiom, "It's not nearly as important what is true, as what the caller thinks is true."

However, we do not wish to give the impression that caller perception cannot be measured to an accuracy sufficient to make difficult decisions. Quite the contrary is true. In a properly designed caller satisfaction survey, we can ascertain the mindset of a population of callers to within an accuracy of 95% allowing managers to make reasonable, consistent decisions from a caller CS program. Accuracy to a 95% level essentially means that conclusions made using this qualitative caller data will be correct 19 times out of 20 tries. Not bad for most decision makers!

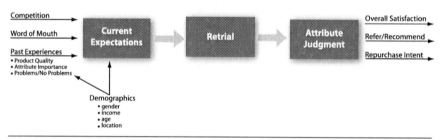

Figure 14. Model of the CS Process

A Model of the CS Process

There are four factors that determine satisfaction with various service attributes, and these in turn influence overall satisfaction, willingness to recommend, and repurchase intention (the three principal global CS measures). The factors are service quality, expectations, attribute importance, past experience (problems/no problems with the service/product), and various demographic variables like type of customer, length of relationship with your products, gender, income, and age. See figure 14 for a diagram of our model of the CS process.

Note these critical features about our model:

1. Service expectations are driven by the segment variables, such as business-to-business versus business-to-consumer accounts, as well as by previous satisfaction experiences. For

example, customers with large monthly accounts may expect a different level of service from the contact center than those with much smaller accounts. Expectations for service are generally formed by past experiences with other contact centers including, but not limited to, your contact center. Expectations are also impacted by word-of-mouth and competitive offerings.

2. Service attributes (or characteristics) have no significant effect on customer expectations. Rather the customers' evaluations of the service attributes combine to create performance ratings. The performance ratings are inputs, which drive the overall satisfaction rating. The effect of the attributes on overall satisfaction will then be derived using regression analysis.

3. We suggest the demographic variables do not usually affect attribute satisfaction directly, but indirectly through expectations and attribute importance. Again, customers who use your larger, more complex products and services or pay larger fees may place more importance on available contact center customer services than other customers, which in turn will influence their overall satisfaction. Consequently, as the CS program expands in the future, the same type of CS analysis can be repeated on the various segmented customer groups to identify differences.

The obvious goal of the CS surveying program is to define, refine, and ultimately provide quality telephonic service for all callers. This does not necessarily mean providing the same level of service for everyone. A bank does not supply the same services at no cost to those with modest accounts as it does for the big investor, but it should strive to provide segment-specific quality service.

Content of a CS Program

Recall from the introduction to this chapter that the CS program will be measuring the perceivable attributes of the telephone service experience. In most instances, there is no point in asking customers about attributes that are not behaviorally actionable. To be behaviorally actionable the attribute factor must be under your control and lead to concrete actions rather than vague ideals. For example, in a university setting, one of the things not under the control of the administration is the amount of paperwork required from students in completing a loan application. This process is commonly viewed as burdened with excessive paperwork, and that

79

lack of control is due to the need to document adherence to outside standards.

In this case, there is little to be gained by asking the students how satisfied they are with the administrative process of applying for a loan. On the other hand, if you are working with federal or state regulators and it is still possible to make some changes to the forms or amount of paperwork, then asking the students how much paperwork they consider "excessive" could be useful.

In general, two parts of the contact center are under management's control and would therefore be measured by the CS program. The first part is the operation of the contact center in the form of the levels of the internal metrics that were described and discussed in Chapter 3. The second part is the people/process/technology issues that enable the level of customer service provided. The customer service attributes comprise the external metrics.

In general, the external metrics that are characteristics of telephonic customer service can be grouped into three categories:

1. Accessibility to the contact center (see Chapter 5 and Appendix E)
2. Interaction with the agent
3. The answer or solution provided by the agent

Contact Center Service Level Attributes

1. Caller perceivable attributes of accessibility:
   - number of rings
   - queue time
   - hold time
   - number of transfers

2. Caller perceivable attributes of the interaction with the agent:
   - handled the call quickly
   - showed concern for the caller's situation
   - understood the caller's question
   - spoke clearly

3. Caller perceivable attributes of the answer given by the agent:
   - completeness of the answer
   - accuracy of the answer
   - fairness of the answer

We will focus on three key indicators or drivers of customer satisfaction:

1. Overall satisfaction with the quality of contact center service experienced

2. Likelihood to continue using the product or service (repurchase intention) as a result of the experience with the customer contact center

3. Willingness to recommend the product/service to others

General Instrument, Data Collection, and External Analysis

In Appendix A, you will find a proven caller satisfaction survey to begin the CS program for your contact center. See Appendix B for a discussion of the Computer Assisted Telephone (CAT) survey system that we strongly recommend for caller data collection. See Appendix C for a discussion of sampling concepts. All three appendices are critical to the efficient and effective running of a contact center CS program. We have provided sufficient detail for those who need a refresher on data collection and sampling.

We recommend reading through Appendix D, which indicates how to complete the external metric analysis through what is called "risk analysis." The goal of risk analysis is to uncover where your contact center runs the possible risk of losing customers so that you can take specific action to remedy the problem before it becomes too costly. An example is provided in that appendix.

Calculating Performance Scores

We recommend re-coding the customer survey responses into a 100-point scale. When presenting results of performance, it is generally easier for the audience to understand the meaning of a 100-point scale. Figures 15 and 16 are common data transformations.

Original Scale Value	Re-coded Value
1	0.0
2	11.1
3	22.2
4	33.3
5	44.4
6	55.5
7	66.6
8	77.7
9	88.8
10	100.0

Figure 15. Transformation of data from 1–10 to 1–100.

Original Scale Value	Re-coded Value
1	0
2	25
3	50
4	75
5	100

Figure 16. Transformation of data from 1–5 to 1–100

After re-coding the original scale, the performance is quantified by calculating the mean for each service attribute, overall satisfaction, willingness to continue service, and willingness to recommend.

The performance scores are important, but they are only part of the necessary management information. Of course performance results pinpoint the service attributes on which the agents receive low scores. However, a more effective analysis would be to determine which service attributes are contributing to the three primary drivers of customer retention:

1. Overall satisfaction
2. Willingness to recommend
3. Repurchase intentions

In order to examine each attribute's contribution to the overall picture, a multiple regression analysis must be conducted. Regression analysis allows all attributes to be considered in a single equation which is a much more attractive option than conducting a long series of correlation analyses repetitively examining the relationships between pairs of variables.

In attempting to define callers' overall satisfaction ratings, we can build a model to include all of the service variables. "Overall satisfaction" is a function of the attributes listed in figure 17. The attributes listed correspond to the surveyed CS items.

The analysis is specifically focused on determining which attributes are affecting overall satisfaction ratings at a statistically significant level. Those attributes in figures 17 and 18, which are statistically affecting satisfaction with the service interaction, are marked by the asterisk (*). These are significant at the 95% confidence level. If that attribute also has a performance score of less than 85, a need for improvement has been identified.

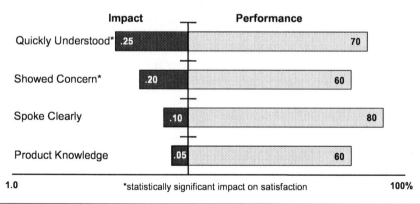

Figure 17. Attribute Performance and Impact—Example 1

A clear presentation of the regression results is critical. We recommend a two-sided bar chart so that the users of the report can see the performance scores along with each attribute's respective affect on overall satisfaction. Figure 17 presents results pertaining to the agent. This is how the multiple regression results should be interpreted:

1. The chart indicates that two attributes are statistically impacting satisfaction: the agent "quickly understood" the customer's situation and "showed concern" for the customer when answering questions. These two attributes then become the focus for management action. Improvement efforts should not be made on attributes that are not statistically impacting overall satisfaction.

2. Looking at the performance side of the chart, it is apparent that neither significant attribute is achieving the desired level of 85.

3. How are these two attributes subsequently prioritized for action? Their respective impacts on satisfaction are close at .25 versus .20. This suggests they are each important to satisfaction ratings and to nearly the same degree. However, the performance scores for the item "showed concern" is at 60 whereas the item "quickly understood" is at 70, so a manager may wish to focus on first improving the scores for "showed concern." It is always wise for a manager to address the issues that require the least amount of financial investment. Gaining small victories is important for the contact center manager, the teams, and the CS program.

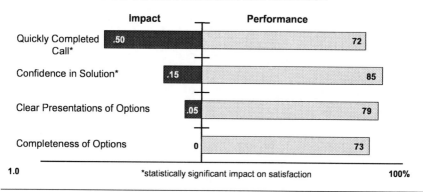

Figure 18. Attribute Performance and Impact—Example 2

The results presented in figure 18 would lead the manager to consider upgrading the training for empathy and listening skills. If you have a quality control team that monitors calls, then they may be able to add yet another perspective. Reviewing the customers' comments from the open-ended survey questions may provide further ideas of what specific agent skills could be improved.

How can you use the results and begin to diagnose the cause for the customers' perceptions? We have constructed figure 19 to suggest some of the general areas of focus when improvement opportunities are identified by the multiple regression and performance scores.

Possible Focus for Improvement if Performance Score is Below 85%	Service Attribute Measured by CS Survey
• listening skills • empathy skills • telephone techniques • product training • communication techniques • telephone techniques • telephone, communication techniques, system improvement • system training, system improvement issue	Agent: • quickly understood customer's request • showed concern when answering questions • spoke clearly • product/service knowledge Answer/Solution Provided: • completeness of answer • customer's confidence in solution provided • clear presentation of options • quickly completed call

Figure 19. Suggested action based upon survey results

Results presented in figure 19 focus on the service attributes of the answer/solution provided. Similar to the above discussion, first focus on the attributes that are statistically impacting satisfaction; i.e., those that reflect caller delight and ultimately, retention. The number of attributes that are statistically significant may be zero or may be all of them. In figure 18, there are two: "quickly completed call" and "confidence in solution."

The impact of "quickly completed call" is apparently much larger than the impact of "confidence in solution." Most importantly, the performance on "quickly completed call" is only 72 compared to the 85 for "confidence in solution." As suggested in figure 18, "quickly completed call" has implications for further system training, or perhaps a system improvement is required. The training is obviously less expensive than a system change, so you may want to begin with the training. If you suspect a system problem and have been attempting to garner support for the upgrade, this information would be valuable to include in the discussion.

The "confidence in solution" attribute is statistically impacting satisfaction and the performance is at the 85% level. This provides the manager with an opportunity to distribute this information about the center. It may become a service differentiator: that is, something around which to build an advertising campaign touting your service as being above that of your competitors.

The changes made as a result of the CS measurement program should be tracked very carefully. When results from the next measurement period are produced, a comparison of the new results to those in figures 17 and 18 will enable the success of the actions to be evaluated.

One other way to present the results of the external metrics plotted in figures 17 and 18 is to place the individual attributes on a matrix as shown in figure 20. With such a matrix, it becomes immediately possible to see where improvement is needed.

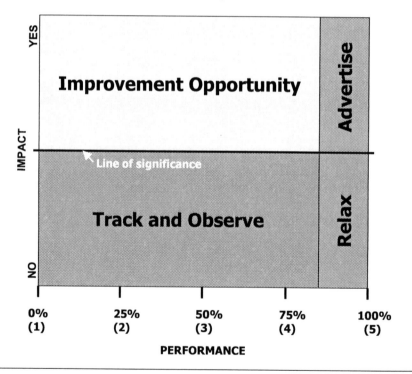

Figure 20. Improvement decision matrix

Customer-Driven Contact Center Management

The ultimate customer satisfaction improvement method is one that allows the customers to define great service. Every customer has opinions, even when no one asks.

Do you know the impact that your call center has on your company image? BenchmarkPortal recently contacted 1,000 U.S. consumers to ask them about their experience with call centers. Ninety-two percent said their experience was important in shaping their image of the company (see figure 21).

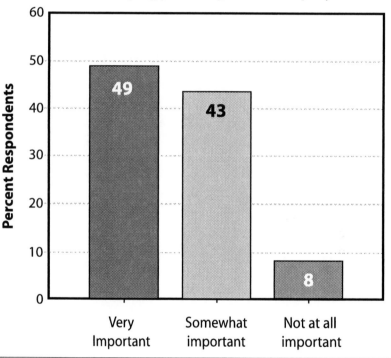

How important was your overall call experience in shaping your image of the company?

Figure 21. Impact of experience on company image

In today's global economy, as markets reach higher and higher levels of saturation, new customers become harder to find. The companies that endure are those that ensure their current customers are not just satisfied—but loyal.

Customer Satisfaction Drivers

In the following illustration, customer needs can be summed up as follows:

Anton's Hierarchy of Caller Needs

Figure 22. Anton's Hierarchy of Caller Needs

By drilling down, these needs can be classified into two primary categories:

- low-value satisfaction drivers:
    o receiving accurate answers
    o having fast access
    o being offered a choice of contact channels
- high-value satisfaction drivers:
    o being treated as unique
    o receiving specific advice
    o regarded as a partner in the company-customer relationship
    o feeling that the company "Knows Me"
    o receiving timely follow-up to their contact

Unfortunately, what many contact centers measure and manage are:

- accurate answers
- fast access
- a choice of contact channels

When what they should be focusing on are:

- treating each customer as unique
- providing specific advice above and beyond their expectations
- regarding each customer as a partner in the relationship
- making the customer feel that the company "Knows Me"
- providing timely follow-up to their contact

What percentages of your customers are loyal? If you're not currently capturing, analyzing, and utilizing the voice of your customer, how do you know? Most companies collect customer opinions at some level, but according to a recent survey, most contact centers don't use the information to improve performance at any level, as shown in figures 23 and 24 below:

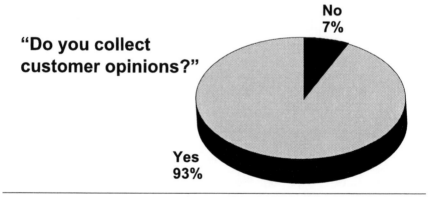

Figure 23. Percentage of companies that collect customer opinions, at some level, on their service

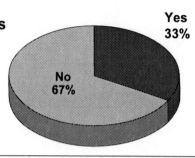

"Do you use the customer opinions collected to influence internal change?"

Figure 24. Percentage of companies that use customer opinions to improve customer service at any level

Tragically, caller feedback is seldom used where it can do the most good...namely changing agent behavior. Yet, many call centers spend a great deal of time and money on call monitoring to improve importance. But research shows that:

1. Too many call centers still rely on the traditional agent monitoring and coaching model as a way to improve customer satisfaction, as follows:

   - five calls monitored randomly per agent per month
   - supervisors use checklist to determine quality score
   - supervisors or QA meets with the agent within 24 hours

2. Even when done well and consistently, this method has marginal impact on customer satisfaction.

3. In summary, the issues are:

   - lack of time to devote to call monitoring
   - lack of experienced people to do monitoring (often your best agents)
   - lack of supervisor time to do coaching
   - not enough calls monitored to get an accurate picture of any one agent

So, why not put the caller to work helping you monitor the quality of their own calls by capturing their opinion, and save head-count and money in the process? What you get in return is a statistically valid volume of feedback straight from the customer, delivered in real-time, to those who can best impact caller satisfaction—the agents.

BenchmarkPortal has developed the ultimate service improvement solution, called *Echo™, "Every Customer Has Opinions"*. *Echo* permits you to do more than just capture customer opinions—*Echo* allows you to use it. By using *Echo*, you can "hear" your customers and use that knowledge to leapfrog ahead of your competition.

The four main components of the *Echo* solution are:

1. **Customer Opinion**
   - direct, focused questions
   - collected by e-mail or after-call IVR survey
   - details by customer type
   - drill down by reason for contact
   - details of why dissatisfied

2. **Agent Behavior**
   - based on best practice findings
   - metrics aligned with true objectives
   - unfiltered feedback directly from the customers they served

3. **Service Recovery**
   - provides instant damage control of dissatisfied customers
   - recovery done by key recovery talent
   - tracks impact of various recovery methods
   - management has details on service break-downs
   - customers resurveyed to ensure final satisfaction

4. **Failed Service Analysis**
   - easy-to-read reporting of drivers of dissatisfaction
   - unbiased details from customers
   - impact versus performance charts
   - trending information on impact initiatives
   - determine effectiveness of products, policies, and processes

Echo utilizes customer surveys to collect satisfaction data that is processed and reported to management on a continuous "dashboard" basis. The following are just a few examples of the reports available to managers through ***Echo:***

Front-line leadership
can access customer satisfaction results
for any team, any time

Overall, how satisfied were you with the way your call was handled?

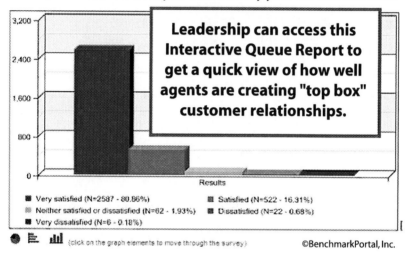

Figure 25. Echo™ Example Report #1

At a high level, Echo shows you what your customers think is important

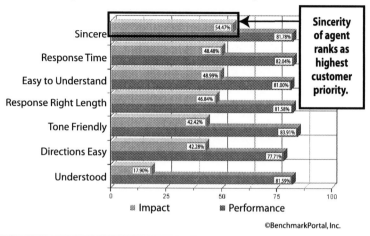

©BenchmarkPortal, Inc.

Figure 26. Echo™ Example Report #2

Ranked by % of customers that were "very satisfied" (top box)

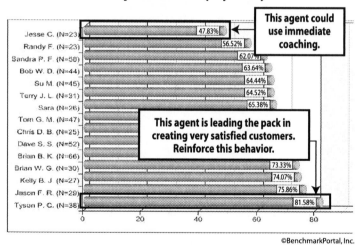

©BenchmarkPortal, Inc.

Figure 27. Echo™ Example Report #3

Its breakthrough features include this real-time dashboard for management plus the ability to trace satisfaction right back to the individual agent. Agents can self-monitor, and coaching becomes focused on the voice of the customer, instead of a sterile checklist.

Agents have instant access to their customers' feedback

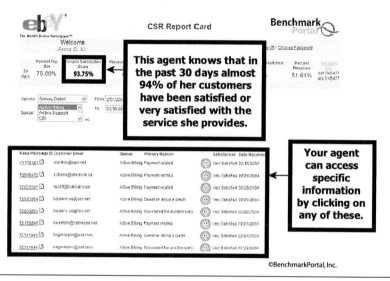

Figure 28. Echo™ Example Report #4

Your agents will see how their performance compares to that of their peer groups!

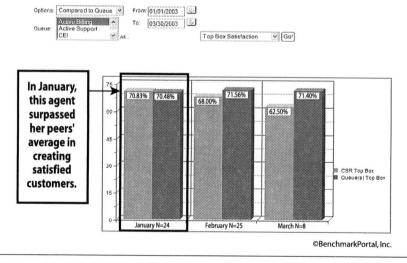

Figure 29. Echo™ Example Report #5

This system truly focuses coaching on teachable moments, rather than old-style, hit-or-miss checklist monitoring.

Finally, **Echo** gives you the ability to "feed" dissatisfied customers in real time to a trigger team of "recovery experts"— essentially agents who can turn a very dissatisfied customer into a very satisfied, and loyal, customer.

The importance of this is shown in the following table:

Effective Service Recovery Pays Off

Customer Situation	Repurchase Probability
Product with no problems	78%
Product with problems and an ineffective Customer Care Center (calls and e-mails)	32%
Product with problems and an effective Customer Care Center	89%

©BenchmarkPortal, Inc.

Figure 30. Echo™ effectiveness table

Indeed, the recovered customer can be an important source of revenues and positive "word-of-mouth" going forward.

This is very high-quality, immediate input that provides high-quality, real-time data for analysis and improvement. Users have experienced dramatic and measurable increases in customer satisfaction and agent satisfaction after adoption of this solution.

Key Contact Center Process Elements

Contact center processes designed from the customer's requirements drive the implementation of new processes as you transform your contact center to better meet the caller's business or personal strategies. Below are listed several key contact center process elements to consider.

1. Strategy and Mission: Would your callers agree with the mission statement for your contact center?

2. Access Points: How does your customer find your 800 number, e-mail address, or Web site?

3. Transmission: How does the call/contact get to your contact center?

4. Disaster Recovery: When disaster strikes, what is the backup to minimize service loss for the customer?

5. Telecommunications Products: What devices are answering your calls/e-mails?

6. Staffing and Scheduling: Does your system match the right agent with the customer contact every time?

7. Education: How are the agents trained and retrained?

8. Tools, Applications, and Databases: Is the data the agent needs quickly accessible?

9. Message Delivery (Scripting): Do the agents get any help from computer-derived scripts as to what to say/write to the caller/contact?

10. Customer Communication Channels: If there is more than one contact center answering calls/contacts from your customers, how are these integrated and coordinated to appear seamless to the customer in need?

11. Metrics and Reporting: Are you measuring the right process at the right time to have available decision-making information when you really need it?

12. Customer Satisfaction: How do you measure the perception that the customers have about the quality of the service you manage?

13. Business Operational Costs: Do you have a handle on all expenses that drive the budget for your contact center, and are these costs available in a timely fashion to allow management action when needed?

14. Facilities: Do you carefully monitor the ergonomics of your contact center to ensure the most efficient and effective workflow processes?

CHAPTER 5: LINKING INTERNAL AND EXTERNAL METRICS—
THE ULTIMATE MANAGEMENT TOOL

Background

Many managers are striving to improve and reengineer their contact centers. From our experience, many of today's contact centers fit into the lower left corner of the matrix shown in figure 31 which could be labeled the "as is" customer service center. These same managers are striving for and have a vision to move to the "to be" customer access center of the future and become a corporate asset.

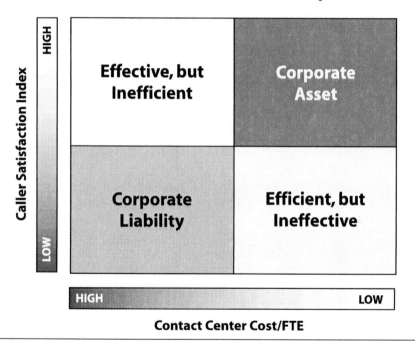

Figure 31. Management matrix for the vision of improvement

It has been our experience in assisting many contact center managers in achieving their vision of the "to be" customer access center, that they first become very effective in terms of achieving high marks in caller satisfaction. Only after that goal has been achieved do they then strive to reengineer the cost out of the system and move to the coveted upper right cell of the contact center performance matrix, as shown in figure 32 below:

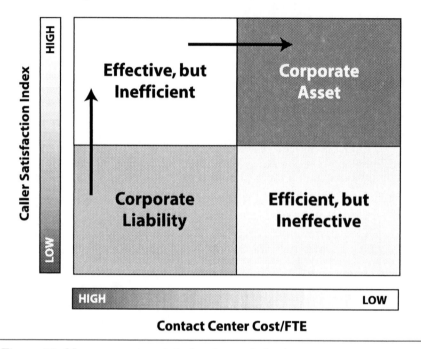

Figure 32. Management matrix for the path for improvement

Figure 31 presents the rationale for combining the cost and satisfaction components. First consider the idea of managing only to reduce cost per contact. It is unlikely that your center will be delivering outstanding customer service, but rather focusing on being productive. Productivity, taking as many calls as possible, may mean efficiency but it does not mean that the center is effective. Effective is successfully engineering each call to maximize the probability of receiving high service scores from the callers. The CS program enables management to address the corporation's demand to focus on cost per contact, but adds a key component called customer satisfaction.[1]

The mission of the contact center then becomes one of movement toward providing value-added customer service at the lowest possible cost per contact as shown in figure 32. The management of the center

---

[1] Delta Dental Plan of Michigan, an organized labor center, accomplished this through an intensive coaching campaign directed towards agents as well as all levels of management.

can be driven toward the vision of the Corporate Asset Center in the upper right cell of figure 31.

The objective of incoming contact center management is to balance the dynamic mix of resources including network services, equipment, and staffing to maximize the ROI of the contact center. This management balancing act must be accomplished while meeting the contact center's operational targets in the areas of quality, productivity, and efficiency. It is, however, important not to let the internal metrics drive management at the expense of the contact center's mission for quality and customer satisfaction.

Service level goals for quality, productivity, and efficiency are usually set by:

1. Benchmarking best-in-class contact centers
2. Reviewing industry averages
3. Previous experiences of the contact center manager

None of these strategies really enable the contact center manager to set operational goals knowing how each will affect the caller's perception of service.

The bars for service achievement cannot be arbitrarily set if the contact center wishes to operate as efficiently as possible while still satisfying caller expectations. The following scenarios are possible outcomes when goals are set without including caller satisfaction analysis:

1. Any or all of the bars could be substantially higher than what the callers are expecting resulting in higher costs without consequent gains in customer satisfaction and loyalty.

2. Any or all of the bars could be substantially lower than what the callers are expecting resulting in dissatisfaction and possible defection behavior.

3. The manager can change goals for service without knowing how caller satisfaction is affected, unknowingly resulting in either higher than necessary costs or defection.

4. The bars may need to be fine-tuned over time as service expectations change, but this will not be detected if caller analysis is not periodically undertaken.

5. All customer groups may be subjected to the same service levels but inappropriately so if segment expectations vary.

In figure 33 below, we have listed the way in which internal metrics are connected to caller perceptions. Using the simple regression analysis described next, the internal and external metrics will be quantitatively linked. The internal/external survey is presented in Appendix E and includes scripting, questions, and identification of the internal metrics to which each question is linked.

Internal Operational Metrics	Customer Perception and Degree of Acceptance
• actual time in the IVR • actual time in queue • actual hold time • actual number of transfers • actual talk time • blocked-call percentage at time of call • abandonment rate at time of call • time to abandonment at time of call • after-call work average at time of call	• perception of the time spent in the IVR • perception of the time in queue • perception of time in hold • perception of need to transfer & agent's product knowledge • spent enough time with agent to resolve issue • how events in the call center affect the call quality of the customers who were served as rated by overall satisfaction and likelihood to continue service

Figure 33. Internal operations metrics and customer perception

This, combined with the data analysis, benchmarking information, and management's previous experience, will provide direction for management's activities. Like all statistical analyses, this technique does not remove the need to think, but rather is a valuable addition to the manager's tool kit.

Simple Regression

The point was made earlier that the customer perception of the operational dimensions of the contact center should be used when setting the bars for service levels. Several types of analyses can provide the manager with strong, quantitative tools to set the service level goals.

We propose the use of simple linear regression models. We will present a highly abbreviated discussion of regression with a single example here. A more detailed discussion with an additional example can be found in Appendix F.

Regression is a technique that produces a model to predict the value of a dependent variable using the values of an independent variable. In this application, the independent variable would be the per call actual internal metrics as captured by the ACD. The dependent variable to be predicted is the caller's perception of each metric as rated using the external CS survey.

The regression technique plots each independent and dependent variable pair. For example, on a set of coordinate axes, one axis would indicate the number of rings that actually occurred with caller #1 as reported by the ACD (say 3), and the other axis would indicate satisfaction with the number of rings as reported by caller #1 in the external survey (say 5). The intersection of those two would provide the unique grid placement of that pair of data values (3,5). All data pairs are plotted and the regression algorithm places a straight line of best fit through the data.

Three types of relationships may exist between the independent and dependent variables: positive (an upward sloping line as viewed from the point of origin), negative (a downward sloping line as viewed from the point of origin) or a line with no slope (horizontal or vertical). One would expect a positive relationship to exist between "satisfaction with spending enough time with the customer" and "talk time." One would expect a negative relationship in situations where a metric, such as "queue time," is too long. Where the two variables show no relationship, the manager can infer that focusing on that metric will not generate a change in satisfaction.

Case Study 1

Situation

Using the regression-simulated results for the variable "time in queue", we would get a Beta (see the definition of Beta in Appendix F), which was positive, negative, or zero which tells us the form of the relationship between the average rating of "satisfaction with queue time" and the average "actual queue time."

Inserting the simulated results into the regression model detailed in Appendix F:

$$69 = 92.27 + -1.3 \ (17.9)$$

where 69 is the average rating of 'satisfaction with queue time' (dependent variable) and 17.9 seconds (independent variable) is the actual average 'time in queue'. The Beta is negative so the relationship is negative.

Management Interpretation

If the "time in queue" was reduced by 1 unit (a second) then the "satisfaction with the time in queue" would increase by 1.3 units (from 69 to 70.3). If the "time in queue" was reduced by 2 units, the "satisfaction" would increase by 2.6 units to 71.6. Therefore, reductions in "actual queue time" are predicted to increase perceptions of "satisfaction" in a dependable relationship of 1:1.3.

We can compare these results to the results for other variables to determine where the least change will result in the most improvement in satisfaction by examining ratios just like the one above (or Beta weights straight from the regression equation). This information can then be combined with estimates of the cost of making the indicated changes to arrive at the optimal managerial decision.

Management Reporting

At eBay, Meg Whitman, CEO, has a simple rule, as illustrated in figure 34 below:

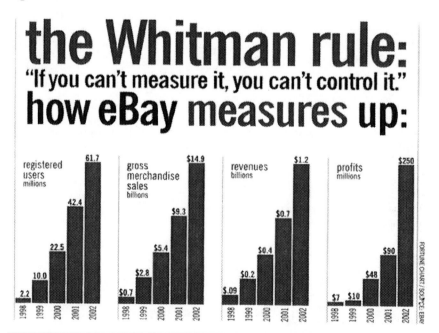

Figure 34. The Whitman Rule: If You Can't Measure It, You Can't Control It.

A manager's information needs can be summed up as follows:

- real-time access to the data
- reports that anticipate their decision-making style
- reports that are timely
- reports that are "actionable"—in short, the report output design gives you a clear hint as to the action to be taken

If you think of yourselves as a pilot that must navigate your business toward its objectives, needing access to a multiplicity of information indicators that you can view without losing your "out of the windshield" focus, how would you feel if your performance dashboard looked like this?

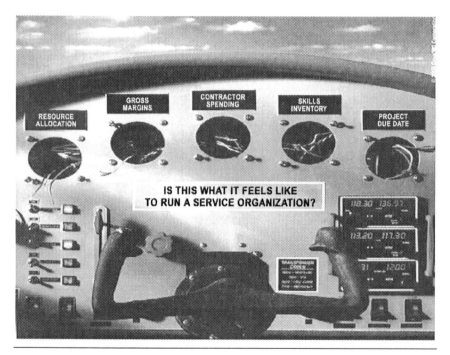

Figure 35. Is this your performance measurement dashboard?

Many times, reports furnish raw information without translating the information into knowledge that we need to make a decision. In other words, they simply are not really "Actionable". The following two charts offer a simple example of what we mean:

Not Really Actionable

Figure 36. Example: Information that is not really actionable

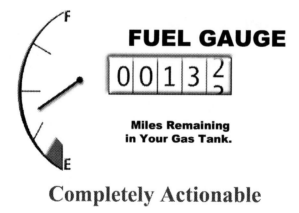

Completely Actionable

Figure 37. Example: Information that is completely actionable

Figure 38 presents a graphical summary of the "big picture" regarding performance management:

Just Having the Numbers Isn't Enough!

Numbers vs. Business Intelligence

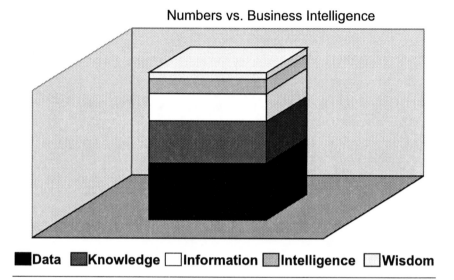

■Data ■Knowledge □Information ▨Intelligence □Wisdom

Figure 38. "Big Picture" of performance management

Performance Report Design and Architecture

In designing "Actionable" reports, you must first consider the audiences that the reports address and the intent of the report:

- individuals = change behavior
- teams = compare performance
- departmental = quality, quantity, balanced score card
- other departments = caller information that assists decision-making:

  o executive management
  o marketing
  o public relations
  o field sales
  o quality assurance
  o legal
  o field service
  o others that are industry specific

Examples of the typical types of "Actionable" reports include:

- Exception - only send if data exceeds a threshold.
- Trend - time based changes.
- Status - snapshot of "as is" condition.
- Statistical - Are the changes statistically different? Use cross tabs for data mining.
- Mapping - overlaying performance over geographic location.
- Diagnostic - drill down to find root cause.
- Data overlays - one plus one equals five in terms of information content.

Examples of reports that are provided to agents to "self-manage" would include:

- caller satisfaction at the agent level
- calls per agent per shift
- occupancy
- adherence
- first time final calls

Performance metrics used by the supervisor to optimally manage a team of agents should include:

- caller satisfaction at the team level with comparison at the agent level
- calls per team per shift with comparison at the agent level
- first time final calls at the team level with comparison at the agent level

Performance metrics required by the "Control Tower" include:

- calls offered versus calls handled
- blockage rate
- maximum delay
- service level
- abandon rate

Performance metrics needed by the data analysts are:

- slice and dice capabilities:
  - o   determine optimal ASA by queue
  - o   determine core causes of dissatisfaction

- expert help hub:
  o number of calls to hub
  o top reasons for calls
  o final disposition of calls

Performance metrics used by the contact center site director to optimally manage a center. For instance:

- all the control tower metrics by split
- budget issues
- specific to Blue Cross—health care:
  o number of adjustments
  o average turnarounds to complete
  o top reasons for adjustments

- NMIS Reporting:
  o performance compared to NMIS' requirements
  o total inquires resolved in 2, 7, and 21 days
  o average delay
  o lost call percentage
  o inquiry accuracy

In summary, to be of value, performance metric measurement and reporting must be timely, accurate, and "Actionable", unlike the example shown in figure 39.

Figure 39. "Is this your idea of an Actionable Report?"

CHAPTER 6: AN ARGUMENT FOR CONTACT CENTER BENCHMARKING

Introduction to Benchmarking

With the emergence of technological advancements that bring product development, marketing, and product distribution to increased highs and capabilities over what was possible in years past, quality customer service becomes the new battleground for corporate America. The paradigm shift moves from best product-quality, to best service-quality, and the establishment of best practices in quality customer service as customers demand instant access to vendors and product manufacturers. These shifts force market leaders to create initiatives that a) increase customer retention, b) maximize the use of customer contact channels, and c) maintain a competitive market share (Call Center Excellence, 2001). Benchmarking performance metrics provide the best method for the customer contact center to measure its efficiency, effectiveness, and its ability to provide quality customer service.

During the days of Opie and Andy of Mayberry, My Three Sons, and Dennis the Menace, the lion's share of customer service was done over the counter top. If the product broke, the customer happily brought it back to the store; when additional information was required about service options, a salesperson could easily assist; and when someone issued a complaint, the entire store would gladly turn its attention to the customer in order to find a suitable resolve. Moreover, customer service had the connotation of someone being up front, personal, and friendly when in need of service from a company. People enjoyed to shop because of the people in the stores who where there to service the customers' needs. This environment allowed a distinguishable measure of customer service.

Unfortunately, those days are gone; the telephone, e-mail, and the Internet have become the new medium for customer service. Although the on-site customer attendant found in most stores remains knowledgeable about the key points of their products, customers are often required to use the company's toll free number to access in depth and detailed information about service contracts and warranties. According to studies at Purdue University and

BenchmarkPortal, by the year 2008, over 85% of all customer interactions with a company will be conducted through the customer contact center via telephone or the Internet. For most companies, this translates into increased service level demands that must be met on a daily basis in an efficient and effective manner.

This traumatic increase in the flow of traffic through the contact center, has moved the requirements of having (in most cases) only a single telephone operator to greet customers and directs calls, to the necessity of a multifunctional contact center that seats hundreds of agents, and support multiple products or the products and services of multiple companies (outsourcers). Aided by the implementation of computer telephony integration (CTI), sophisticated workforce management software, quality monitoring, and a host of other technological advancements contact center management can:

- develop proactive and strategic management styles

- implement initiatives that lead to greater customer satisfaction

- provide customer differentiated by product or service needs

With the addition of multimedia access channels like e-mail and Internet Web Services to a new wave of customer relationship strategies, the traditional contact center has evolved into a customer contact center that is highly automated and technology-enabled. Customers who once called the traditional agent-intensive inbound call center are now greeted by interactive voice response (IVR) units, computer telephony integration (CTI), or may access the contact center through a variety of self-service Web applications. This enriched form of customer contact provides customers with a greater sense of control and promotes higher levels of customer loyalty. However, there are some adverse conditions of automation. Some customers claim that automation removes the human touch from customer relations and thus reduces the desire to communicate with vendors.

Moreover, technology advancements in the customer contact centers produce an overwhelming amount of performance data that is available to managers and analysts. This performance data becomes the measurable metric utilized in the benchmarking operations. Contact centers are dynamic; the workload varies with the pulse beat of the customer. Managers cannot schedule when the work will arrive to the center, only plan according to a forecast based upon a historical report. Managers who monitor contact center metrics can often develop an understanding of the following customer characteristics:

- frequency of unique contact
- who is contacting the center
- major and minor reasons for contact
- tolerances for waiting a response by either phone or e-mail

Contact center managers who do not monitor the performance metrics of their centers, may be managing their centers out of a job. According to Dr. Anton:

> "It is entirely possible for a call center to perform so poorly that customers become dissatisfied simply by virtue of the contact with the call center, thereby increasing the likelihood that they will disengage from your company's product or service at the next available opportunity. Such a call center would be a corporate liability (see figure 31)."

As Director of the Purdue University Center for Customer-Driven Quality, and the preeminent worldwide lecturer and spokesman of contact center excellence, Dr. Anton defines benchmarking as "a structured and analytical process of continuously identifying, comparing, deploying, and reviewing best practices worldwide to gain and maintain competitive advantage."

Revered as the leading authority in contact center benchmarking and customer relationship management (CRM), Dr. Anton has over fifteen years of study in contact center benchmarking and is the author of more than 22 books and 96 papers on customer service and call center methods. One significant point in Anton's definition, is that he refers to benchmarking as a continuing process; this implies that multiple iterations of the benchmarking process may be required before metrics may be sufficiently compared, reviewed, and deployed as best practices.

Another significant point of consideration in Dr. Anton's definition is that of structure; the accurate collecting of contact center data for a measurement against data collected from a group of peers, in order to gain an apples-to-apples comparison of best practices, requires the structured format of an industry standard. It becomes increasingly apparent, that the process of benchmarking requires time and a study of the KPIs that lead to best practices.

The classification of contact center metrics falls into two categories: internal metrics and external metrics. Internal metrics are the hard numbers produced by the computers, telephones, auto-dialers, automatic call distributors (ACD), voice response units (VRU), and internal departments such as Human Resources. External metrics, often referred to as soft metrics, are the qualitative analysis; they represent the feelings and sentiments of the customer.

Sources for collecting contact center performance data include: ACD, integrated voice response units (IVR), automated e-mail management systems, voice network services, data network services, line monitoring, adherence monitoring, and computer-assisted telephone/e-mail surveys. When properly and consistently measured, recorded and tracked, and processed into actionable reports, managers can take those actions that will offer initiatives to improvements within the contact center, increase the levels of customer satisfaction, and a promote return on investment for the contact center.

Examples of internal metrics include:

- adherence to schedule
- after call/contact work time
- average abandonment time
- average cost per call/contact
- average handle time
- average hold time
- average e-mail response time
- average speed of answer
- average talk time
- number of calls/e-mails per 8-hour shift
- agent occupancy
- percent of calls closed on first call
- percent of e-mails resolved on first contact
- percent of contacts resolved in IVR
- percent of contacts resolved by e-mail auto-response
- percent of contacts resolved by Internet chat
- percent of contacts resolved by Internet self-service
- cost per contact
- sales per contact

An example of external metrics include:

- queue time
- hold time

- number of rings before answer
- number of transfers
- completeness of answer/response
- accuracy of information in answer/response
- level Of communication
- willingness to recommend
- willingness to repurchase or use services again
- overall satisfaction with product and/or services offered

During the benchmarking process, a collection of data points (performance-metrics) are gathered for the purpose of measurement against like data coming from other contact centers. An index of performance standards, based upon the weighted averages of collected contact center data provides the standard for measurements. Contact centers thus measure the delta or gap between their metric values and those of the index, which serves as an industry or peer group standard. This is benchmarking in its simplest form and for the contact center it establishes a reference point on performance measures.

Although there are various forms of benchmarking, two forms are predominant: high-level industry benchmarking and peer group benchmarking.

High-Level Benchmarking

High-level benchmarking involves benchmarking against the averages of groups from one or more of the following types:

- the contact centers from various industries
- contact centers from within the same industry
- best contact center in various industries
- direct competitors in the same industry

This type of benchmarking is intended to provide a snapshot view of their call center for one of the following purposes:

- establish a baseline prior to an improvement initiative
- performance/benefit validation at a predetermined point (3-6 months), following implementation of an improvement initiative
- semi-annual checkup of overall call center performance
- establishing justification for an improvement initiative

- producing call center performance reports for higher management

One of the best high-level benchmarking programs is *RealityCheck™,* a quick and easy program offered on a free basis at the BenchmarkPortal Web site (www.BenchmarkPortal.com). RealityCheck™ offers a number of option choices for both inbound and outbound customer service and technical support call center operations. RealityCheck™ instantly shows how your center is performing. After completing our short survey, RealityCheck™ compares your call center's performance to other centers, and ranks your call center in both efficiency and effectiveness. The ranking is displayed on our "Balanced Performance Matrix" graph. An example of this matrix can be seen in figure 40 below:

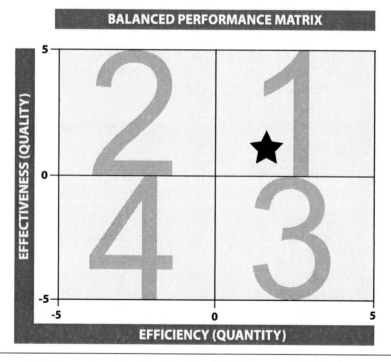

Figure 40. Example of the RealityCheck™ Balanced Performance Matrix

So what are you waiting for? It's fast, easy and free! And you get results immediately after submitting your data online. Get started today at www.BenchmarkPortal.com!

Peer-Group Benchmarking

Benchmarking against a peer group provides data at a significantly more granular level than any high-level industry benchmark. The concept of peer group benchmarking may be directly related to a visit to the doctor for a routine, annual check up. During the visit, the doctor will collect a sampling of data points such as blood pressure, age, height weight and a myriad of others; generally about thirty nine in all. From this, the doctor measures the data collected against an index derived from peer group information (i.e. age, race, ethnicity, height, and weight) and derives a picture of health; peer group benchmarking follows much of the same methodology.

Common delimiters used in defining a peer group include:

- industry sector
- contact center size in terms of agent workstations
- number of agents (full-time and part-time)
- number of contacts handled by the center (annually)
- percent of contacts outsourced
- agent functionality: customer service, order taking, technical support, reservations, sales, call routing, etc.
- audience: business to business, business to consumer, internal customer
- contact flow: inbound versus outbound

In an ideal benchmarking scenario, the target center shares the exact same characteristics as its peers; however, this does not always occur in the peer group benchmarking process. Furthermore, it is common for companies to feel that only companies of the same industry or industry type are suitable as peers for benchmarking. Using the following example, it becomes evident that companies of disparate types become comparables in the benchmarking initiative.

The value of understanding the peer group composition is demonstrated through the following example displayed in figure 41:

Call Type	Your Company	Medical Blood Supply	Automotive Insurance Co.	Beverage Bottling Co.
Inbound	Yes	Yes	Yes	Yes
Customer Service	Yes	Yes	Yes	Yes
Dispatch	Yes	Yes	Yes	Yes
Outbound Follow-up to Inbound Calls	Yes	Yes	Yes	Yes

Figure 41. Benchmarking peers

In figure 41, the medical blood supply company, automotive insurance company, and the beverage bottling company each perform pre-sales and post-sales (customer service), send people to resolve issues on site (dispatch), and do follow up calls to order requests (outbound calls as follow up to inbound calls). Each of these companies is uniquely different from each other, yet they share in the same peer group.

For example, the medical company sells a liquid; it ships a liquid, and it dispatches people to fix dialysis machines. The beverage bottling company sells a liquid; it ships a liquid, and dispatches people to fix dispensing machines. The insurance company sells a product, supports the product, and dispatches road repair. Each of these companies executes the same types of functionalities in their center, thus making them functional peers for best practice benchmarking.

The objective of peer group benchmarking is to establish the positioning of the contact center against its peers in terms of efficiency and effectiveness. Here again, the logic is simple. Contact centers that are both efficient and effective in respect to their peers, may progress towards being a corporate asset; however, contact centers that are less efficient and less effective than their peers at performing the same tasks, could become a corporate liability. Additionally, by calculating the gap between a contact center and its peers, managers can understand the metric to dollar relationship that affects the bottom line.

Continuous Improvement: Benchmarking at Your Best

Contact center managers get the biggest improvements in operations, the greatest increases in customer satisfaction, the biggest boosts to their careers (and the careers of their contact center colleagues) and the largest increases to their company's bottom line when they make benchmarking part of a continuous improvement process, in which they are able to demonstrate measurable improvements in competitive performance quarter after quarter, year after year.

Our studies indicate that, in many sectors, the average tenure of a contact center senior manager is about two and a half years. The idea is to make benchmarking an integral part of your management and budgeting process. The commitment to multiple benchmarks has numerous advantages, including the following:

- A rigorous benchmarking program assists center managers in getting the attention and approval of their top-level managers. They will react positively to a well-structured program that gives them quality information about a vital corporate function.

- By emphasizing a journey over time toward world-class excellence, this approach admits up front that the first attempts may show more problems than strengths for a contact center. *You are not expected to be perfect* from the start! You *are* expected to be working towards best in class, balanced excellence over time. Your company will reap the rewards and you will have something to show senior management at bonus time for yourself and your people.

Imagine the added managerial power and real-life results that this program can afford. Then subscribe and start the journey toward success.

Contact Center Certification: Enhance Your Career While Adding Value to Your Company

Our vision for raising the collective performance of the contact center sector has led naturally to endeavors that go beyond management of the center. These endeavors include contact center certification.

The continuous improvement benchmarking discussed previously finds its culmination in certification. Contact centers in search of excellence must commit to a process that involves:

- bringing your contact center up to measurable best practices standards

- maintaining those standards over time

- training your people to optimize their skills in support of best practices

Centers that attain upper-right quadrant status on our Peer Group Performance Matrix (figure 42) have achieved a balanced score card of performance (efficiency and effectiveness) and are eligible for certification. These centers can ask us to come on-site and audit and validate their inputs.

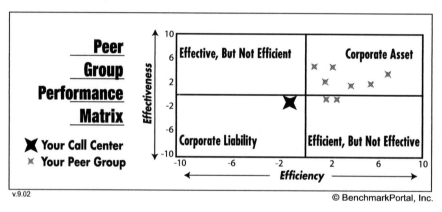

Figure 42. Peer Group Performance Matrix

Our research has also shown that the upper right hand quadrant indicates that a center is the *low cost provider* for its mission (figure 43). All other quadrants represent a higher cost situation and require action to achieve optimization.

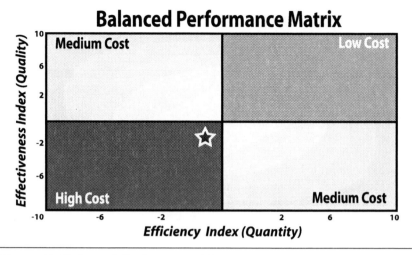

Figure 43. Balanced Performance Matrix

Thus, improving your operations is also in the best interest of your company.

Contact Center Assessment - Getting a second opinion

Contact centers are a company within a company. As stated in the introduction of this book, contact centers have an obligation to their stakeholders to provide a reasonable service at a reasonable cost; however, in most cases the contact center is prejudiced by being perceived as a cost center and is not measured for the value of the service it provides. Thus, the obligations of the management team include the challenges of raising awareness to the mission of the center, establishing credibility and value for the center within the organization, and gaining executive support.

To this point, we have looked at benchmarking as a management tool designed to assist managers in their daily navigation through the seas of contact center operations. We discussed many of the types of data available for collection to include internal and external metrics, and various benchmarking methods and expressed the value of making benchmarking an integral part of a continuous improvement process of the center. Although the continuous measurement of performance gaps between ones own metric values and the values of ones peers and/or industry for the same metric pinpoints certain areas where improvement is needed, most managers do not have the time nor expertise to engage into a discovery process leading to a root cause analysis of each gap. For these reasons, getting external help by an independent non-bias third party is best.

The age-old and most common methods for getting a second opinion on the performance of the center and to troubleshoot the bugs, is to call upon the services of a consultant; however, who should one call? The answer to this is easy, go with whom you feel the most comfortable. There are numerous networking groups or communities for contact center professionals that are loaded with resources of these types, and the (independent) consultants associated with these groups are eager for work. In addition to this, most major hardware and software product vendors either have a product-specific consultant channel or may have a referral to consultant services in your area. A key point to remember with both the independent consultant as well as the vendor-related consultant is that they are usually tied to a specific process or solution. An alternate solution that allows you to stay in the driver's seat is offered by BenchmarkPortal in its contact center assessment process.

Our qualification process is unique in that it rests on the world's largest database of pertinent metrics. Thus, while it fosters best practices and process improvement, it is fundamentally tied to measurable, quantitative *results*, results that spell the real difference between success and failure.

BenchmarkPortal's Center for Customer-Driven Quality Certification is the ultimate recognition of contact center excellence against a competitive background. As such, it is a step that enhances the careers of those deserving people who help achieve it. The most sought-after managers in this industry are those who have achieved certification. The most respected companies are those whose contact centers have gained this distinction.

BenchmarkPortal's assessment and certification program is unique in that:

- It is a program that offers clear objectives that are *measurably* value enhancing against a competitive landscape.
- It is supported by a complete menu of top quality training and assessment opportunities that light the way toward improvement, and ultimately toward certification.

The assessment and certification process contributes to all of the fundamental objectives indicated in the first chapter:

- exceptional visibility into operations using *measurable metrics*, not just process analysis

- operational improvement and enhanced work-like environment

- enhanced career development, opportunity and reward for managers and their people

- improved shareholder value through improvements to the bottom line

At BenchmarkPortal, certification is a key goal of the benchmarking assessment and certification process.

Certification also is an important point of pride for a call center and can be leveraged by management to:

- boost morale of call center personnel

- increase respect for the call center within the enterprise

- give greater credibility to budget requests for improvement initiatives

The Assessment and Certification Process

Research shows that there are at least sixteen processes tied to each telephone contact with customers and each performance gap is but a reflection of a break in one or more of these processes (see figure 44). BenchmarkPortal's assessment process, which is a value-add of its Center of Excellence certification processes, provides managers with an in-depth discovery of these processes.

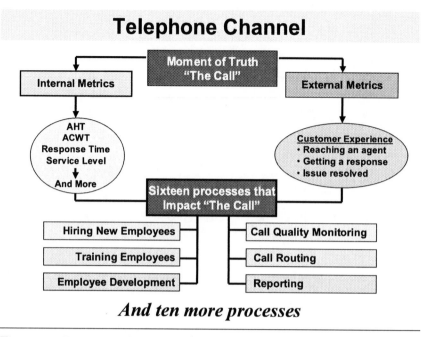

Telephone Channel

Moment of Truth "The Call"

Internal Metrics

AHT
ACWT
Response Time
Service Level
↓
And More

External Metrics

Customer Experience
• Reaching an agent
• Getting a response
• Issue resolved

Sixteen processes that Impact "The Call"

Hiring New Employees

Training Employees

Employee Development

Call Quality Monitoring

Call Routing

Reporting

And ten more processes

Figure 44. Processes that impact the call

The assessment process follows two basic steps: First, a benchmark report is produced to discover your performance gaps against the averages of your peers and your industry. An in-depth survey of your IT and organizational structure is conducted for a performance analysis, and third, a consultant, certified by BenchmarkPortal, Inc., and the Purdue Center for Customer-Driven Quality visits your facility to validate the data you submitted and perform a discovery into each gap, the processes and sub-processes relating to each gap.

Telephone Channel

Processes affecting "The Call"	
Hiring New Employees	Call Quality Monitoring
Training Employees	Call Routing
Employee Development	Reporting
Real-Time Expert Help	Call Center Performance Evaluation
Employee Compensation	Caller Satisfaction Measurement
Service Improvement	Caller Service Recovery
Knowledge Access	Employee Internal Communications
Workforce Optimization	Caller Self Service

Figure 45. The processes affecting a call

Agent turnover, as an example, is a constant pain point to most managers. In wrestling with this pain point, a common course of action by managers is to leave the issue with their Human Relations (HR) department. Some HR departments are extremely pro-active. Often, incentives are offered to agent's who refer others for employment with the company; company picnics are held, and "wellness" campaigns are developed to promote a positive corporate culture. As an end-result and when all else fails, temp agencies are often utilized to find the "right type of people" for the center. However, in their book *Minimizing Agent Turnover,* Anton and Rockwell (2001) point out that the lack of opportunities for advancement within the organization is a leading cause for voluntary attrition among agent's.

The specific processes requiring of in-depth discovery for improving the gap in agent turnover include:

Agent Hiring Process, which includes the following sub-processes:

1. Best practices in recruiting

2. Best practices in on-line screening

3. Best practices in aptitude testing

4. Best practices in skill testing

5. Best practices in behavioral interviews

6. Best practices in top talent analysis

7. Best practices in determining agent pay scale

8. Best practices in effective exit interviews

9. Best practices in temporary to permanent hiring processes

Call Monitoring and Agent Coaching Process, which includes the following sub-processes:

1. Best practices in recording calls

2. Best practices in who should do the monitoring

3. Best practices in monitoring frequency

4. Best practices in what to monitor and score

5. Best practices in monitoring calibration

6. Best practices in agent coaching

7. Best practices in relating monitoring to agent development

8. Best practices in using caller feedback in the monitoring/coaching process

Agent Real-Time Help Hub, which includes the following sub-processes:

1. Best practices in real-time agent hub development
2. Best practices in real-time agent hub deployment

Agent Compensation, which includes the following sub-processes:

1. Best practices in determining competitive compensation
2. Best practices in launching a pay-for-performance system

Agent Development, which includes the following sub-processes:

1. Best practices in determining competitive compensation
2. Best practices in agent mentoring
3. Best practices in agent training
4. Best practices in agent coaching
5. Best practices in career-path development
6. Best practices in leadership training

From this list it becomes evident that the areas of opportunity for the investigation of a gap in turnover are numerous. Aside from validating the benchmark data, the function of the consultant during the on-site engagement is to connect the dots between the gaps and those processes affected. The results of this Sherlock Holmes approach of discovery, a piece-by piece walk through the center, is a report containing an analytical review of the current state of the center and recommendations for improvement, which includes graphs, charts, and tables, developed and delivered in an executive presentation. The choice on how to engage thereafter is the decision of contact center management.

Using sample data, the following graphics display samples of a typical report of findings and recommendations stemming from an on-site discovery.

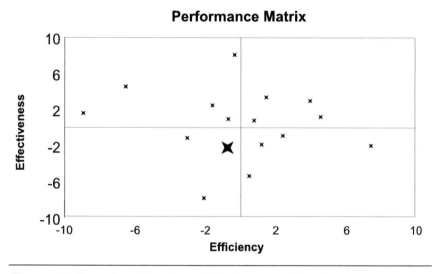

Figure 46. Sample of Benchmark Performance Matrix

A Balanced Score Card For Sample Company

Peer Group Performance Matrix reflects a "balanced scorecard" of effectiveness and efficiency metrics; metrics are weighted to yield composite score. Below is a sampling of key metrics:

Effectiveness Metrics	Your Value	Industry Average		Efficiency Metrics	Your Value	Industry Average
Top Box C-Sat in Percent	67.53	62.50		Average Inbound Calls/Agent/Hour	9.00	8.52
Top Box A-Sat in Percent	73.20	68.10		Calculated Self-Service in Percent	35.00	22.90
First Call Resolution	85.74	71.40		Calculated Cost per Call in $	4.23	5.46
Bottom Box C-Sat in Percent	3.50	2.24		Calculated $/FTE	87,635.00	80,173.00
Bottom Box A-Sat in Percent	15.47	11.23		Average After Call WorkTime in Minutes	1.50	1.33
Average Speed of Answer in Seconds	25.00	20.10		AverageTurnover in Percent	22.00	29.60
Calls Transferred in Percent	9.00	4.00		Average Talk Time in Minutes	2.53	3.10
HoldTime in Seconds	42.00	28.90		Agent Utilization in Percent	64.00	77.89
Abandoned in Percent	3.28	2.99		Agent Occupancy in Percent	85.00	88.30
80% of All Calls answered in Seconds	35.00	22.50		Calculated $/Minute	1.12	0.89
Average Time in Queue in Seconds	35.00	25.40		Adherence to Schedule in Percent	88.00	93.50
Calls Blocked in Percent	2.00	2.10		Average Attendance in Percent	93.00	95.60
Opt Out of IVR in Percent	5.00	21.40		Average Aux Time in Percent	15.00	12.34
Avg. Time before Abandoning in Seconds	27.00	62.80		Agent /Supervisor	28.00	17.34

Figure 47. Sample of Balanced Score Card Report

Findings and Recommendations related to Agent Turnover

- Finding: High agent pressure within the local area (over six competitive centers).

- Predominately use employee referrals and local newspaper. Have explored using local college.

  o Recommendations: Investigate and refine the current recruiting methods and hiring processes.

  o Develop an exit interview process to discover why people leave.

  o Develop opportunities for advancement within the center and organization, i.e., Team Leads, Supervisors, etc.

Benchmark  A Datamart of Best Practices™
Portal

Figure 48. Sample of Assessment Findings and Recommendations

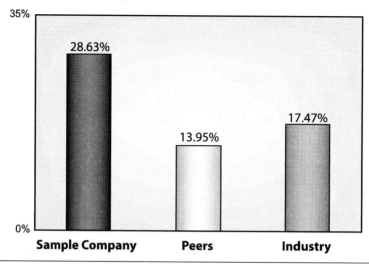

Figure 49. Sample of Gap Analysis: Agent Turnover in Percent

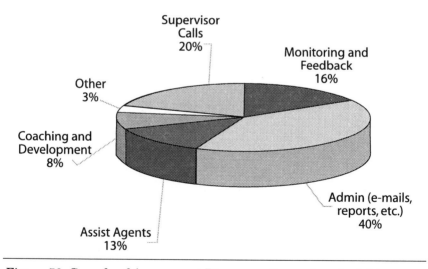

Figure 50. Sample of Assessment Discovery: Supervisor Activities

Next Steps

- Decide on an agent retention strategy

- Pick top one to three alternatives that best fit the strategy

- Begin an initiative to develop a business case for the top alternative

- Develop suggestions for short-term improvements regardless of ultimate solution

Benchmark Portal   A Datamart of Best Practices™

Figure 51. Sample of Assessment Next Steps Recommendations

The deliverables at the conclusion of the assessment process include:

- an executive debriefing of the engagement findings
- peer group performance matrix
- performance benchmark audit analysis
- next steps recommendations to achieve **Center of Excellence** certification

If you have achieved **Center of Excellence** status, then you:

- are awarded the **Center of Excellence Certificate** (see figure 52) and banner that attest to your center's achievement and which can be displayed prominently at the center itself
- continue best-practice processes and improvements

©BenchmarkPortal, Inc.

Figure 52. Sample of Center of Excellence Certificate

Certified centers are honored at the annual Call Center Campus industry event and usually choose to celebrate their success with ceremonies and social events for call center personnel.

Centers that achieve certification work to sustain it over time. This has a salutary effect in terms of continuous improvement and fostering a best practice environment.

Conclusion

As mentioned previously, benchmarking requires a structured approach. Managers and analysts should seek out qualified advice from certified professionals before starting any benchmarking initiative.

Moreover, it is important to understand that benchmarking is a tool, and that it alone does not guarantee success of the contact center. It is applicable however, to every aspect of customer contact within the contact center to include:

- process knowledge
- human resources

- workforce management
- quality monitoring/assessment
- customer satisfaction
- performance measurements

Through benchmarking, managers can pinpoint areas where improvement is needed, create initiatives that lead to increased performance in the contact center, enhanced customer satisfaction, reduced costs, improved competitive advantage, and increased market share.

CHAPTER 7: MANAGING TO INCREASE CONTACT CENTER ROI—CUSTOMERS AS CORPORATE ASSETS

Referring back to the customer lifetime value calculations (CLV) introduced in Chapter 2, it is possible to look at customers as corporate assets and attach a value to them. By association we can attach a value to the contact center that provides a level of telephonic service that delights the caller into a state of loyalty. Note that it is entirely possible for a contact center to perform so poorly that customers become dissatisfied simply by virtue of the contact with the contact center, thereby increasing the likelihood that they will disengage from your company's product or service at the next available opportunity. Such a contact center would be a corporate liability as shown in the lower left cell in figures 42 and 43.

As we illustrated in figure 5, those callers who score 85 or higher on a caller satisfaction index (or CSI) are "delighted" and have a high probability of remaining loyal customers who continue to purchase our products and/or services. These customers are highly likely to resist competitive offers, while at the same time spreading positive word-of-mouth to others. Those who score a CSI of 50 or less are dissatisfied and are likely to actively seek to disengage while spreading negative word-of-mouth to others about their poor contact center service experiences. All of that word-of-mouth is likely to generate at least some influence; that is, some people will be influenced by what they hear and act on that influence.

Defining Return on Investment (ROI)

Every chief executive officer has a fiduciary duty to maximize the return on every dollar of capital available to the company. With intelligent analytical information on customers and your CRM system, you can begin to make ROI calculations. Therefore, with a limited supply of capital for investments in process enhancements, every proposal for capital expenditure must be accompanied by a complete financial analysis demonstrating the possible return to the company of the proposed investment. Many times people tend to avoid trying to do these kinds of calculations because they know that the numbers they have to work with are estimates. For most C-level executives, a well thought out estimate is better than nothing. Most

CFO projections are just that; so don't be afraid to venture into ROI land.

Everything is measurable. It is really about putting a stake in the ground, gathering as much information from as many experts surrounding you and then presenting it with an open mind to get feedback. In introducing the ideas behind ROI, we will focus on a call center in the following section to help the ideas of ROI become grounded in reality so that you can use them.

There are classically two ways to approach an ROI endeavor: direct costs and profits from revenues generated.

Cost Reduction and/or Cost Avoidance

"Direct costs" are those expense items that can be directly attached to a product or service offered by the company, and that can also be easily tracked by the company's accounting system. Indirect costs are those less tangible costs not as easily tracked by the accounting system and therefore often lumped together as overhead.

Focusing on direct costs is the most common approach to ROI calculation and, in our case, of call center information/telecommunication technology investments. Some common direct cost savings are:

- increased productivity allowing fewer agents to do more in less time
- implementing information technology that replaces the agent's function altogether
- reduced telephone costs due to less time-in-the-wait queue

ROI calculations of this type are common, straightforward, and will not be discussed herein, even though we strongly recommend that they be used in conjunction with the ROI calculation techniques discussed below.

Profits from New Revenues Generated

This approach works well for some call center investments. It focuses on the simple concept that certain enhancements in customer service will result in retaining more customers, and also that retained customers will continue to purchase from us and produce profits. Our example below will focus only on this approach, since it is subtler and less often taught in MBA or other business education programs.

Prepare yourself for some resistance and criticism in this category of cost/benefit analysis, because some financial professionals find this approach more difficult to accept, less tangible, more difficult to measure or hard to tie directly into the project being considered.

A Combination of Savings and Earnings

The combination of savings and earnings is nice, but one important design rule in calculating ROI is "keep it simple" for the audience to understand and to believe.

By assisting your client in presenting a credible and well-documented ROI, you are substantially increasing the probability that the company you are consulting with will actually implement your suggested call center enhancements. Ultimately, "hard dollar" ROI arguments are what sell new technology investments. The approach that we are doing "good things" for our customers, also known as "soft money," frequently does not convince top management to take action.

Revenue Elements to be Considered

From our call center baseline survey research, we will have determined the process where the company's performance is low and where the impact on customer satisfaction is high. The model that we need to develop for the company is, "If we invest in and improve the selected process, what will the increase in customer loyalty and repurchase be worth in dollars and cents?" The data we need to determine added income value from this customer is:

1. The average number of purchases made each year, and the profit margin per purchase
2. The average number of years that a customer remains loyal to the company

Cost Elements to be Considered

The cost elements are determined by:

1. A bill of materials with costs of all the pieces of the proposed information technology
2. A cost estimate of the labor charges to install, train, and maintain the information technology investment
3. The cost of capital over the lifetime of the information technology to be implemented

In Section 6, on becoming more CLV-centric, we will show how an ROI can be calculated for certifying via best practices at a CRM interaction center.

ROI Model Assumptions

As in all financial models, there are basic assumptions that drive the model and affect the final results. Any and all of the assumptions below can be changed to meet your intuitions without changing the concept of this kind of financial modeling. Our assumptions are as follows:

1. We assume that a Caller Satisfaction Index (CSI) of 85 or greater indicates that a surveyed caller was delighted.

2. We assume that each time a customer calls your call center and is delighted by the experience, loyalty is maintained and customer lifetime value (CLV) re-earned. For the purposes of our ROI model, we will give the call center full credit for protecting the CLV of each delighted caller.

3. We assume a positive word-of-mouth factor of 5 to 1, and a positive impact factor on prospective customers of one new customer for every 100 prospects told about the call center experience.

4. We assume that a CSI of 50 or less indicates that a surveyed caller was very dissatisfied and will most probably disengage from your company at the next possible opportunity.

5. We assume a negative word-of-mouth factor of 20 to 1, and a negative impact factor on prospective customers of one lost prospect for every 50 prospects told about the negative experience.

6. We assume that we can extrapolate from the percentage of the surveyed callers that rate their call at 85 or more or 50 or less to the whole population of callers. This basically indicates that we are confident that the sampling algorithm is valid, which means that the sampled population represents the universe of all customers that called your call center.

7. We assume that each target customer group will most probably have a different CLV.

8. We assume that the cost of a company's call center is fixed at a period of approximately one month.

9. We propose calculating the ROI on a monthly basis.

Inputs Needed to Use Our Model

1. We need the CLV for each target customer segment.

2. We need the percent of callers surveyed by target customer segment where the CSI was 85 or higher.

3. We need the percent of callers surveyed by target customer segment where the CSI was 50 or lower.

4. We need the total number of callers by target customer segment by month.

5. We need the total cost of the company's call centers by month.

Calculations Performed in Our Model

1. We determine the number of loyal customers generated by target customer segment by multiplying the surveyed percentages by the total population of callers in each target customer segment. To determine the value of these loyal customers, we multiply the computed totals by the CLV for each target customer segment. The sum total of all segments gives us the value of the total positive revenue stream produced by the superior quality of service delivered by your call center.

2. We determine the number of disloyal customers generated by target customer segment by multiplying the surveyed percentages by the total population of callers in each target customer segment. To determine the lost value of these dissatisfied customers, we multiply the computed totals by the CLV for each target customer segment. The sum total of all segments gives us the lost revenue stream produced by the inferior quality of service delivered by your call center.

3. By adding the results of one and two above we know the net revenue stream produced by your contact center during the month in question.

4. To determine the ROI for your call center, we take the net revenue for the month and subtract the net cost for the month and divide this number by the net cost for the month. To convert ROI to a percent, we multiply the result by 100.

A Simple Contact Center ROI Example

For the sake of illustration, let us demonstrate by continuing with the CLV example developed in Chapter 2. In this case, we are assuming only one target customer.

A Simple Call Center ROI Example

Input Data From Call Center Metrics:		Value	Calculations
Customer Lifetime Value	=	760	
Percent with CSI > 85	=	5	
Percent with CSI < 50	=	2	
Total Calls per Month	=	1,000,000	
Computed Values			
Loyal Customers Generated:	=	50,000	(1,000,000 x .05)
Positive Word of Mouth Factor: 5:1	=	250,000	(50,000 x 5)
Positive Influence Factor: 100:1	=	2,500	(250,000 / 100)
Customers Lost	=	20,000	(1,000,000 x .02)
Negative Word of Mouth Factor: 20:1	=	400,000	(20,000 x 20)
Negative Influence Factor: 50:1	=	8,000	(400,000 / 50)
Net Gain (or Loss) of Customers	=	24,500	(50,000 + 2,500 - 20,000 - 8,000)
Computed Gain (or Loss) of Revenue	=	$18,620,000	
Computed ROI for the Call Center			
Total Revenue Gained (or Lost)	=	$18,620,000	
Assumed Cost of Center	=	$15,000,000	
Return on Monthly Investment (ROI)	=	24%	(((18,620 - 15,000) / 15,000) x 100)

Figure 53. Simple call center ROI example

In figure 53, it can be readily seen from these computations that the call center can be a strong generator of revenue from delighted, and therefore loyal, customers. It can be an especially potent weapon in highly competitive and volatile industries such as telecommunications, financial services, and the like.

A More Complex ROI Example

Now let us consider a more complex contact center ROI example with four different customer segments that contact the call center. Notice that all the numbers come together in figure 54 to provide you additional performance measures: i.e., total revenue gained (or lost) plus contact center ROI. You will find that executive management of your company is much more likely to understand a financial analysis of performance than simply a report or graph showing internal metrics derived from ACD data.

A Complex Call Center ROI Example

	Business Units			
	One	Two	Three	Four
Input Data Listed by Business Unit				
Customer Lifetime Value:	$8,000	$3,000	$6,000	$10,000
Percent with CSI Exceeding 85:	5	10	4	2
Percent with CSI Less than 50:	3	1	1	3
Total Calls per Month:	70,000	60,000	30,000	65,000
Computed Values by Business Unit				
Loyal Customers Generated:	3,500	6,000	1,200	1,300
Positive Word-of-Mouth Factor:	175	300	60	65
Customers Lost:	2,100	600	300	1,950
Negative Word-of-Mouth Factor:	840	240	120	780
Net Gain (or Loss) of Customers:	735	5,460	840	-1,365
Computed Gain (or Loss) of Revenue:	**$5,880,000**	**$16,380,000**	**5,040,000**	**($13,650,000)**

Market Gain (or Damage) Simulator

Computed Market Gain (or Damage)

Total Revenue Gained (or Lost) Monthly	$13,650,000			
What if the Total Centers Monthly Cost is:	$10,000,000			
Return on Monthly Investment (ROI):	37%			
What if the Percent Delighted Were:	5	10	4	2

Figure 54. Complex call center ROI example

A "What If" Question for the ROI Model

What would happen if we were successful in increasing the number of callers with a satisfaction (CSI) rating of 85 or more by just 1% in each target customer segment? What would that be worth to your company? When we rerun the ROI model simulator for the last example (see figure 55), the increase is almost $17,000,000, and the ROI goes up from 37% to over 200%. Even making this example more realistic by increasing costs (which would certainly happen if new processes, technology, additional training, or agents were put into place to accomplish this increase in CSI rating) would leave an impressive result. This is "proof positive" that investments in contact center customer service can have a major payback as long as we pick the areas most valued by the callers. Of course that was the focus of Chapters 4 and 5. The connection here is that if the regression analysis discussed in Chapter 5 and shown in Appendix F forecasts an increase in overall customer satisfaction, you can now connect it back to calculate revenue gains and ROI improvements from the contact center.

Market Gain (or Damage) Simulator

Computed Market Gain (or Damage)

Total Revenue Gained (or Lost) Monthly	$30,135,000			
What if the Total Centers Monthly Cost is:	$10,000,000			
Return on Monthly Investment (ROI):	201%			
What if the Percent Delighted Were:	6	11	5	3

Figure 55. "What If" ROI example

CHAPTER 8: WORKFORCE MANAGEMENT AND MEASUREMENT

Purpose of Workforce Management

Workforce management plays a different purpose depending on various perspectives. It plays a key role in the overall performance of any call center, including increasing efficiencies and reducing costs.

According to a recent *Gartner Marketscope: Workforce Management Software for the Call Center*, workforce management (hereinafter referred to as "WFM") should be reviewed for any center with greater than 50 agents.

> "Call center outsourcers, financial services, travel, hospitality, telecommunication providers, retailers and e-commerce companies are some of the most frequent users of call center WFM software. It is not uncommon for enterprises using WFM systems to report that they achieved the following:
>
> - reduced the time it takes to create agent schedules by 45 to 90 percent
> - increased service levels by 10 to 13 percent
> - decreased payroll costs by 10 to 13 percent
> - decreased call-abandon rates to 3 percent
>
> Overall call abandonment rates consistently average around 7 percent; however, the best performing 25 percent of desks average only 3 percent abandonment, according to Gartner."

Executive Perspective: Support and Enable the Quality Customer Experience and Engaged Agent Culture

The executive's perspective is to create an optimal operating environment while delivering exceptional service to the company's customers. Here are some of the factors related to workforce management that are critical to executives:

- balancing cost, service and quality
- improving the consistency of operational results

- providing resource planning that allows the operation to meet the customer call requirements

- effective long term planning and budgeting

- allocation of time for quality assurance, training, coaching and meetings

Operational Management Perspective: Ensuring the Right People in the Right Place and the Right Time...the Right Way

The management responsible for the daily operation view the purpose of workforce management as providing a valuable tool to help them manage the day-to-day operation. Here are their critical factors:

1. Creating schedules that optimizes the best mix of shifts or schedules that comes as close to the optimal business requirements model as possible

2. Provide a variety and mix of schedules to meet agent work and life balance

3. Allocating time for quality assurance, training, coaching and meetings

4. Supporting the full-time and part-time agent mix

5. Reducing chaos in the call center

6. Balancing the workload

Agent Perspective: Providing Some Discipline to the Way Schedules are Managed. Allowing for Performance Review and Development

To the individual agent, a WFM system can be viewed as either another element of a "big brother" system, or as another tool, such as a recording system, to help gauge their personal effectiveness—especially on the efficiency-related metrics. Their perspective is tied to how WFM is introduced and how it's used in the center. The best approach is when they are involved in the design and processes.

Best in class examples have demonstrated the importance of agents understanding the business requirements and how the scheduling tools are used to ensure that the center's goals and objectives are being met. The agent should be provided real-time or near real-time information on their personal performance utilizing some form of a "score card" or "dashboard" which provides them with both their individual goals and their actual performance. They should also have access to team "score card," in order to compare their achievement to the team.

The Importance of Culture

Most organizations have developed unique cultures. Each culture is reflected in their shared values, norms, beliefs and expectations, in their policies and procedures, and in their view of authority relationships.

We found that the call centers that deployed workforce optimization rather than simply the "management of schedules" (a.k.a., traditional WFM), are part of a larger company culture that recognizes the role of the front line agent as critical to delivering the "exceptional" service experience required to differentiate products. The benefits these organizations reap from adopting the new focus of workforce management extend far beyond efficient schedules, and directly impact their bottom line profits and earnings per share.

On the other hand, the companies that still focus on a more hierarchical command and control culture are continuing with original WFM. In this type of culture, there are still great efficiencies to be gained with the WFM optimization tools. However, the opportunity for greater employee satisfaction is often missed along with the related benefits to the customer and ultimately, the bottom line.

Recommended Corporate Culture Best Practices

Mission statements provide the focus for strategic planning goals and objectives, and help shape the values and the culture of the organization. Mission statements of world-class organizations typically express the goal of providing the best customer service in the business.

A mission statement example from a world-class organization delivering superior customer service:

> "To be the undisputed leader in world travel. We are passionately committed to excellence and to the highest levels of customer service."

The role of WFM is to support the mission of the organization. The best centers understood the impact they had to the overall success. They considered their contribution by having personalized mission-statements, such as:

- developing and retaining a highly skilled and motivated team
- optimally providing the needed skills to service our customers with a consistently excellent level of service

Although it may sound trite, the workforce team is a daily display of "commitment to continuous improvement." It is their role to continuously improve the call center performance from one period to the next.

We will continue to repeat an underpinning in the world-class companies that we visited. In these organizations, all managers treat their front-line agents just like their customers—with courtesy, respect and responsiveness.

The Importance of Change Management

When a WFM system is initially introduced, there is typically some resistance because it brings change.

The most critical aspect of managing this change is education. Before the changes of the agent scheduling process are made, education and communication are critical. First, agents and the entire management team should understand why change was needed and what the benefits are for both the company and the agents.

One of the single most effective tools in the education of the call center team is to understand and see graphically what happens to the average speed of answer (ASA) when any number of agents are absent, and to understand the effect on customer satisfaction and efficiencies which can result in higher costs.

Ideal Components of a Workforce Management System

An ideal workforce management system should:

1. Forecast the arrival rate of incoming contacts and the amount of work (handle time) the contacts will generate for each period (typically 15 or 30 minutes) of each day.

2. Convert call volume forecasts into the number of agents required for each period of the day to handle the incoming contacts within predetermined service level goal.

3. Develop staffing schedules that optimize the balance between agent availability and expected call volumes for each time period during each day to meet the service level goals.

4. Adjust staff schedules as each day progresses to account for actual contact arrival rates along with agent attendance and adherence to their schedules in order to meet the service level objectives.

5. Interface with the automatic call distributor (hereinafter, "ACD") to track and collect statistics regarding incoming calls, including:

   • when the call arrives

   • how long members wait in queue before their call is answered

   • how many members abandon (hang-up) their call

   • how much time agents spend talking to members (average talk-time)

   • how much time agents spend completing work resulting from the call, after the call is completed (after-call work time or wrap-time)

   • real-time statistics on call volumes and queues

   • statistics on agent login/logout status

6. Maintain a historical data base of contact volumes, arrival rates, peak periods, average handle times, minimum and maximum number of hours for each schedule type, and rules determining how weekend and holiday shifts are to be assigned. For instance:

   • part-time shift lengths must be at least four hours, but no more than six hours

   • part-time employees must be scheduled to work at least 20 hours, but no more than 30 hours per week

   • full-time employees must be given either five 8-hour shifts, or four 10-hour shifts per week

   • meal breaks should occur no earlier than three hours, but no later than five hours after the shift begins

7. Use sophisticated forecasting algorithms, such as Erlang C (or an Erlang C derivative) to:

   • generate accurate call-volume forecasts

143

- develop optimal agent staffing schedules

8. Produce schedule and staffing forecasts, using the historical data collected, by skill group and contact type, predicting the resources required to meet the service level goals.

9. Permit management to define the rules for creating agent schedules, including rules for the:

    - minimum and maximum number of hours for each schedule type. For instance:
        o part-time shift lengths must be at least 4 hours, but no more than 6 hours
        o part-time employees must be scheduled to work at least 20 hours, but no more than 30 hours per week
        o full-time employees must be given either five 8-hour shifts, or four 10-hour shifts per week
        o meal breaks should occur no earlier than 3 hours, but no later than 5 hours after the shift begins

    - rules determining how weekend and holiday shifts are to be assigned.

10. Allow agents to specify their scheduling preferences, including:

    - days, and hours within each day, they are available
    - start and/or end time preferences
    - special needs or requests

11. Produce a broad range of reports that:

    - detail the forecasts and schedules for management, supervisors and agents
    - compare actual results to forecasted results

12. Support the use of e-mail, messaging systems, and browser-based tools for agents to obtain their schedules.

13. Balance the needs of agents with the needs of management to cost-effectively serve their member and prospect needs within established service level goals.

The best practices in the workforce management cycle are described within each component in this section.

WFM optimization is made up of four key steps when viewed in general. The four steps do not always occur sequentially as some are ongoing processes that span the life of the workforce cycle, while others take place at different key junctures in the workforce cycle. As illustrated in figure 56, the four-step process is comprised of:

1. Data collection
2. Forecast generation
3. Plan generation (requirements and schedules)
4. Measure results and analyze how to improve

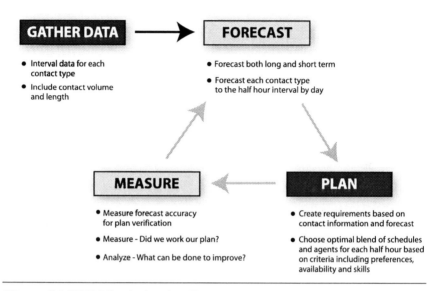

Figure 56. WFM Optimization Steps

Data Collection

No matter what the final method used to forecast and schedule a call center, data collection is a fundamental process that cannot be overlooked. Even in organizations where schedules are fixed, routine monitoring of agent and overall center performance represents a basic data gathering routine. In the truly optimized organizations, data collection is the virtual backbone to operating the call center, in both a real-time and predictive fashion.

Most WFM software packages are tightly integrated with call management systems to eliminate the need for manual intervention in the data collection process. This also allows for the collection of more types of data including critical call volume data, such as arrival pattern data (calls by interval and by day), as well as agent behavior and performance data. Also, data regarding average handle time (AHT) by interval allows for forecasting to account for subtleties such as variances in agent proficiency by time of day and day of week. WFM optimization allows for mitigating under and overstaffing based on the use of averages across all times of the schedule.

Data collection is an ongoing process that, although automated, is augmented with manual manipulation and alteration by the central workforce team. The need for this intervention is driven by non-recurring events that shape call arrival during isolated periods of time. As an example of such an event, if a VRU malfunctions for 2 days and allows all callers to enter the queues, an artificial increase in calls during that period can influence forecasts inaccurately for the period of the forecast algorithm even though the event was isolated and would not predictably occur again. Only via functions that manually normalize the data will forecasts remain accurate.

Forecast Generation

The Forecast Algorithm

Forecasts are the result of the customer call data from recent history being run through a forecasting algorithm. The forecasting algorithm is a mathematical formula that translates historical call data, seasonal influences, and manual adjustments into a prediction of total future calls, call arrival patterns by interval, as well as AHT by interval.

WFM optimization departments from best practice companies have used logic, knowledge of their industry and constant analysis and experimentation to arrive at an algorithm that consistently generates accurate forecasts. Many factors go in to how the forecasting algorithm is formulated. In a quick overview, the common variables that best practice WFM departments account for include:

1. How many weeks of data should be run through the algorithm to include in the forecast?

2. How much "weight" should be given to each week in the forecast—the order of emphasis will depend on your industry, your call flow design and on experimentation?

3. Seasonality—most call centers have variable call volume based on the time of the year due to drivers in their industry and consumer base.

4. Company controlled call drivers—mailings, e-mail blasts or other marketing efforts scheduled to take place will have potentially huge affects on call volume. Best practice

146

organizations track response rates to market stimuli in order to accurately predict future behaviors.

5. Current abandon rates—as fewer calls are handled, logically, more future calls are required and anticipated.

Also, each company had other variables unique to their call centers that they tracked and were mathematically included in each forecast they ran. Also, most companies concurrently tracked forecasts generated by multiple permutations of their algorithm and tracked the resulting forecast accuracy of each side-by-side before deciding the make-up of the current algorithm. One company runs multiple forecasts routinely that are based on differing algorithms to continuously monitor the need for updated or new calculations.

Upon generation of the forecast, the resulting data predicts the number of calls by interval and by day, the length of calls over the same periods, and also required staff to handle the calls.

The requirements calculation contains a critical variable that carries a profound impact on the scheduling outcome. The combination of shrinkage or scheduling overhead with the predicted calls and call length gives the truest possible picture.

Plan Generation—Requirements and Schedules

After determining scheduling requirements, the next step is generating the schedules. If forecasting and requirements calculations were performed in an application outside of the WFM software, as many of the companies in this study do, this data must first be imported before schedules can be generated.

Best in class-WFM software will process the requirements data along with any scheduling constraints necessary to complete the scheduling process. These constraints may include elements such as agent availability, and agent preferences. The companies participating in this study normally generate schedules at least one week in advance. The companies that use schedule bidding generate their schedules far less frequently. This is done for agent consideration, rather than for scheduling efficiency. However, no matter how often scheduling is performed, intra-day elements such as breaks, lunches, meetings, and training can be updated at any time based on real-time variations in business conditions. Unforeseen surges in calls or a high number of agent absences foster the need for such real-time flexibility.

Centralized versus Decentralized Scheduling

Some companies use a distributed schedule generation process, whereby call center team members at their various sites produced individual agent schedules. Other companies chose to keep the responsibility for schedule generation within their centralized WFM team.

Because each option carries with it both strengths and weaknesses, there is no "right way" to create schedules. The distributed method offers the flexibility for on-site management to continuously update and change schedules intra-day. The centralized scheduling method allows for dedicated individuals to use their expertise to foresee the WFM impacts of all scheduling decisions, but does carry with it the open access for easy agent communication.

Forecasting and Scheduling Alternatives

There are a variety of various scheduling tools available in the marketplace. They vary from simple tools with low start-up cost to a significant investment of time and capital for the more automated, flexible workforce management tools.

When starting up or redesigning a call center you must first define the goal/objective in scheduling. Much of this depends on the mission, size, and geographical structure of the call center organization. Once you have planned the objective you are ready to invest in the right technology that meets your call center's needs the first time.

Many organizations have invested in expensive tools only to have not used them properly and have been disappointed in the outcomes. This is typically a result of faulty planning, unrealistic expectations or implementation problems, or a product that does not match the business requirement.

Excel Spreadsheets

The most common form of staffing estimation and schedule generation is performed with a Microsoft® Excel spreadsheet. The reasons for this are many. Excel has become ubiquitous in businesses and users are comfortable with extending the use of Excel to add formulas, macros and even Erlang calculators.

While there are many drawbacks to this methodology, the greatest are:

1. Excel for scheduling is often very labor-intensive and it can be very inexact.

2. This simplified scheduling methodology lacks any skills-based capability and calculation.

3. There is a complete inability to track schedule adherence.

4. No ability to account for random call-arrival patterns.

5. One small error in a formula or macro calculation can be an error that carries forward indefinitely. Who is validating and verifying the inputs?

Users of Excel for forecasting should be calculating seasonality and/or keeping weekly data for year over year trending. ACDs typically store only 13 months of data. There may be a significant benefit at some future time to have weekly statistics (including call length) in an Excel worksheet.

Best Practices for Simple Excel Based Scheduling

The following steps should be taken when using Excel to calculate staffing requirements and to generate schedules:

1. Gather call data. This data can be gathered at a monthly, weekly, daily, or preferably at the interval level (typically 15 or 30 minute intervals). Validate and verify data.

2. Forecast future call arrival patterns. These forecasts can only be done at the level the data was gathered (i.e., if data was gathered at a weekly level, forecasts can only predict weekly call arrival). There are data points available at the network level that can provide at least hourly call distribution. You will have to contact your network vendor to access this data.

3. Estimate required staffing and schedules based on these basic call patterns (e.g., heaviest on Mondays if calls normally peak at the beginning of the week).

4. Be certain to note "special condition," i.e., a special promotion, weather, national crisis, business event, and more.

It should be noted that this method is time-intensive and does not account for frequently changing call patterns. Due to the time necessary to change a large number of schedules, call centers using Excel for scheduling often rely on fixed schedules against an ever-changing call arrival pattern. One typical outcome of this method of scheduling is a center that often misses its key performance indicators (KPIs) goals. In order to avoid this, centers tend to be overstaffed to compensate for the inefficient allocation of a fixed human resource supply against a variable call demand pattern and as a result incur higher operating costs.

Excel spreadsheets for scheduling typically are not effective past 35 to 50 agents depending upon the complexity of the center operations.

Benefits

- inexpensive tool to use
- most computer users have experience in setting up and using formulas
- easy maintenance

Drawbacks

- does not allow for random call arrival
- does not apply skill based capabilities
- adherence is not tracked
- multimedia is not traceable
- no ability to provide flexible schedules
- higher operating costs

Excel with Erlang

Erlang formulas calculate staffing requirements while accounting for random call arrival. These inexpensive formulas can be purchased as an add-on to Excel.

Scheduling with Erlang and Excel accounts for random call arrival so they more accurately estimate staffing requirements. However, because the forecasting and scheduling methods remain unchanged, this method still is labor-intensive, cannot track agent adherence to schedule, and does not account for the efficiencies gained through skills-based call routing

Benefits

- inexpensive tool
- most computer users have experience in setting up and using formulas

- formulas are easily changed
- allows for impacts to be displayed based on volumes entered

Drawbacks

- does not apply skill based capabilities
- adherence is not tracked
- multimedia is not traceable
- cannot input time off schedules
- does not track actual calls

Workforce Management Systems

There are many specific WFM software options. Each of these software solutions is designed to perform:

- call and agent data gathering
- forecasting of future call demand
- calculating agent staffing requirements based on forecasts
- generating schedules to closely match the forecasted requirements
- analyzing the accuracy of the forecast as well as agent adherence and/or conformance to schedule

The benefits of WFM software deployment are quite obvious on the surface. First, WFM software solutions are almost always designed to be integrated with the telephone and automatic call distribution (ACD) system so that the vital process of data gathering can be automated. Since the process routinely requires no human intervention, a variety of robust data elements can be gathered and made available when creating forecasts. The collected data can also include agent level data that provides the ability to track performance by the workforce with regard to schedule adherence and conformance.

Armed with accurate and up-to-date information, WFM software may then provide schedules that meet the demands of the agents, by using individual agent schedule preferences that meet the demands of the business and by closely matching the available staff to the predicted call arrival patterns.

The software often provides other benefits such as the flexibility to update schedules frequently, meeting call demands that change weekly, daily, or even hourly. Some systems even allow for schedules to be changed intra-day based on an unforeseen increase in call demand or a high rate of agent unavailable time (e.g., absenteeism, tardiness, and unscheduled meetings). Many WFM tools can also account for multi-site or multi-skill efficiencies—providing a truer allocation of staff and a reduction in overall staffing costs.

Benefits

- Provides the ability to get measurable results and track improvements.

- Improved accuracy of schedules.

- Increased agent productivity (utilization).

- Reduce supervisory/management time involved in the schedule management processes.

- Automation of workforce management tasks such as data collection and manipulation of the data.

- Reduction in workforce shrinkage.

- Reduction in network costs.

- Can be integrated with payroll systems.

- Schedule Flexibility—for requesting overtime shifts, time off without pay, bidding on shifts etc....the direct supervisor need not be involved in these decisions. An additional benefit is the entire scheduling process is perceived as more fair by the agents. This is a system making the decisions, not a supervisor or manager.

Drawbacks

- If the users are not properly trained in the tool, the tool will not provide them with results that they are expecting.

- The data being entered must be accurate (garbage in/ garbage out).

- There are multiple steps that need to be taken in the software in order to complete the transaction. If you miss a step your data will be inaccurate.

- Validating what the system is doing. Because of the complexity of the software, double-checking what you have asked for is correct.

- The tools that are being offered vary by supplier and do not necessarily support everything that a workforce manager needs to do. Many are creating tools outside of their main tool for validations as well as features that are currently not offered.

Considerations

After seeing the long list of benefits that WFM software solutions produce, most of the drawbacks of utilizing WFM software to forecast, schedule and analyze are difficult to find.

The only obvious drawback to WFM software solutions is that they carry a large price tag. The expense of the systems is not limited to the software, but includes the ongoing cost of supporting and maintaining the hardware and the initial cost of systems deployment. Yet, the money saved by WFM software is substantial. Many of the software providers can provide ROI calculators. Make sure to utilize these tools before making the investment.

Many companies experience other problems that aren't so easily anticipated. Some call centers experience a decrease in employee satisfaction after deploying WFM schedules. This decrease is typically due to a lack of communication and understanding of what the WFM tool can do for the quality of the agent's work and personal life balance. *It is critical that prior to adoption of these methodologies that significant communications with the agents take place.* The agents' performance is now measured in ways they weren't previously. Agents in centers experiencing this issue reported feelings of "big brother" watching over their activities. Culture change and training are key success factors in implementing WFM.

As the channels of customer interactions becomes more diverse (e-mail , Web-chat), the inability of most WFM solutions to gather, forecast, and analyze anything other than phone calls becomes a larger drawback.

Some notes regarding the use of WFM software:

1. The data gathering process must be continually audited to ensure accuracy.
2. Even though WFM software is an automated solution, the system's activities and calculations require validation and maintenance. These duties must be performed by a staff member with a high level of expertise in the WFM discipline to achieve the full benefit.

3. Most WFM software solutions operate at a level of complexity that requires multiple steps processes in order to complete its functions. This dictates the need for a dedicated person or team to ensure full compliance with the business processes that support the systematic processes.

4. No single WFM system meets all goals fully. Each solution has its strengths and weaknesses.

Using our call center benchmark database of key performance metrics, we did a data run comparing those companies with WFM installed versus those that did not have WFM installed.

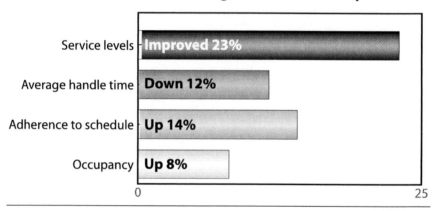

Which metrics did workforce management solutions impact?

Figure 57. Impact of workforce management solutions

Figure 57 shows the impact of workforce management on the key performance metrics, namely:

- service levels improved by 23%
- average handle time down 12%
- adherence to schedule improved by 14%
- occupancy was up 8%

Recommended Best Practices

It is our conclusion that WFM plays an important role in call center efficiency and effectiveness. By taking the improvement percentages shown in figure 57, and assuming a 100-agent call center, taking 1,000,000 calls per year, the cost saving quickly approaches $500,000 per year. This amount of cost saving should produce a very significant ROI for WFM users.

Analysis—Measuring Performance and the Plan

The last step in the WFM optimization process is the analysis of the overall performance—not simply the performance of the call center and its agents, but also the performance of the WFM team, the forecast they generated, the requirements they calculated, and the efficiency of the completed schedules.

Key metrics in the analysis of the agent performance include schedule adherence, which indicates how closely the agents followed the plan and schedule. Another important metric is conformance or compliance, which measures the amount of total scheduled activity completed, regardless of when it was completed.

Metrics used to analyze the performance of the plan vary greatly from company to company. Generally, the metrics include these key performance indicators:

- forecast accuracy percentage
- schedule efficiency
- full time equivalent (FTE) variance from forecast

Regardless of whether the schedules are produced weekly, monthly, quarterly, or even yearly, the analysis of the plan and the collection of data are continuous throughout the WFM optimization process.

Follow the forgoing processes, and you will begin best practice in workforce management.

Summary of Best Practice Perspective on Overall Purpose of WFM

Having observed companies with outstanding results in customer and employee satisfaction, it is obvious, that WFM is no longer about simply *"managing schedules."* The processes and activities have moved to a new level, and the discussion revolves around forecast accuracy and optimal schedules which meet BOTH the business needs and the agent needs in balancing their work and personal life. It's about balancing employees' work-life balance.

CHAPTER 9: QUALITY MONITORING AND COACHING

Companies that do quality monitoring best have created a culture where the agents want to be monitored and coached, and where the supervisors want to be coaches and mentors. In these organizations, there is ample staff and time dedicated to getting the job done properly.

This is in stark contrast to most situations where the quality monitoring and coaching is considered to be a necessary activity, where it is mandated by others and done only when time allowed. In such call centers, there generally is insufficient staff to get the job done. And if call volumes increased unexpectedly (as they often do), the monitoring staff is back on the telephone delivering customer service. The quality process is, as usual, put on the back burner.

The Importance of Change Management

As a company first implements quality monitoring, an essential first step is to get the agents, supervisors, and coaches on board with the concept. The realization that "my work can be scrutinized at any moment" may not be readily embraced by the agents. When not properly positioned, monitoring can feel very negative even to the hardworking, well-intended agent.

At call centers where the quality monitoring process is not properly implemented, negative feeling expressed by agents include:

- They (monitors) are only trying to catch me doing something wrong.
- I do not do as well when I am being watched.
- I get very nervous when someone is watching me work.
- I am being policed.
- I feel like "big brother" is watching me.

At centers that have adopted and used best practices, the agent's feelings are noticeably different. Their reaction to quality monitoring and coaching includes:

- I look forward to my weekly coaching sessions because it shows that my supervisor really cares about my success.

- I enjoy monitoring my own calls; it is amazing to see what I can improve.

- The time dedicated to evaluating my calls tells me that management really believes in its quality mission.

- The coach always gets me involved in analyzing my own calls, and this helps me better understand what is expected.

- I respect my coach and appreciate it when she shows me examples of ways to do things better.

Purpose of Quality Monitoring

On a practical level, most call centers typically conduct quality monitoring to measure agent performance and/or for agent development reasons.

Agent Performance Measurement Only

A small percentage of companies we recently benchmarked currently use only the quality monitoring scores as an agent performance measurement. Supervisors use the results of the scored calls as a representative snapshot of an agent's performance. Each month agents are provided with the summary results of their sampling. Annual merit raises and/or periodic bonuses are based on the score.

Agent Development Only

Some companies use the quality monitoring results as an agent development tool only. The supervisor's focus is on cultivating the skills necessary for their agents to deliver consistently excellent service.

In this environment, the primary metric is customer satisfaction. The quality monitoring and coaching is designed to reinforce behaviors that delight customers and to modify behaviors that don't. The monitoring and coaching score is considered an important, but secondary metric only from the perspective that it could have an impact on caller satisfaction.

Agent Performance and Development

The majority of companies we benchmarked said that they used quality monitoring for both agent performance assessment and agent skill development. These companies viewed the purpose of quality monitoring as the means to ensure customer delight.

Recommended Best Practices

In terms of quality monitoring, we noted the following differences at the world-class call centers:

- The monitoring and coaching function was properly staffed. It was not regarded as an "as available" basis.

- Most agents in these centers looked forward to being monitored and coached because there was positive reinforcement for modifying their behavior to better serve the customer.

- The agents frequently took an active role in discovering what they could have done better and skill deficits were looked upon as training opportunities. Specific training modules were available for almost every skill deficit discovered. The agent's mindset in these call centers was *this makes me a better agent.*

Call Monitoring and Recording Options

Once companies are clear about the purpose of quality call monitoring in their organizations, the next decision becomes: How will we gather the information? Following are the various call monitoring and recording models we documented in the discovery phase of our study. We follow-up each description with its corresponding benefits and drawbacks.

Silent Monitoring—Remote Location

In silent monitoring, the supervisor (or other assigned team member) listens to an agent taking a customer's call in real-time from a remote location, usually within the call center.

Benefits

- The calls are selected randomly. The aim is that the randomness of the call selection will fairly represent the agent's strengths and improvement needs.

- The agent is usually unaware that the call is being monitored, which fosters a more natural call handling. This allows the supervisor to observe the uninhibited interaction between the agent and the customer.

- Monitoring can be done from the supervisor's workstation or from any other remote location, such as another call center, or even from home.

- Silent monitoring at remote locations allows for the establishment of a dedicated, centralized quality assurance team. This team is able to observe calls at all centers within an enterprise to ensure consistency in the application of standards and the rating of results.

Drawbacks

- Providing immediate feedback is typically a challenge.

- This option can be inefficient, as the supervisor experiences unproductive time while waiting for a call to arrive.

- If the agent disagrees with the supervisor's evaluation of the call, there is no "hard evidence" to review as the calls have not been recorded. Disagreements between the agent and the supervisor can be irreconcilable.

- The fact that no recording exists means that the organization has lost the opportunity to share examples of agent excellence for training purposes.

Side-by-Side Monitoring

In side by side monitoring, the supervisor sits beside the agent and listens while the agent handles a customer call. The supervisor also observes the way the agent utilizes available technology and other workstation resources.

Benefits

- The immediacy of providing agent feedback is this option's greatest benefit. It is widely accepted that the closer the feedback is to the actual situation observed, the more potent the learning opportunity.

- This option allows agents to practice more effective behaviors immediately under the guidance of the supervisor.

- The supervisor can observe the agent's use of technology and other workstation resources. Often times, the complexity of information and software available to agents can be a hindrance until it is well understood. The supervisor can facilitate the agents' understanding of available resources.

- Side-by-side monitoring is an excellent option for new hires. Ideally, it is highly interactive and provides an encouraging and supportive environment.

- Questions can be answered, standards can be communicated, and training opportunities can be identified in a conversational manner.

- This option helps establish a personal relationship between the agent and supervisor. This bonding facilitates trust and enhances the agent's confidence in him or herself and between the supervisor and agent.

Drawbacks

- Agents may feel inhibited or threatened and may not perform in a natural or comfortable way. Their true abilities and limitations may not be revealed.

- Observed agents may be on their best behavior; their performance may not reflect their typical behavior.

Call Recording

In call recording, the supervisor or an automated system randomly records calls. The supervisor then listens to the calls and evaluates the agent's performance.

Benefits

- The agent does not know that he or she is being monitored. This scenario provides a more natural example of the agent/customer interactions.

- Agents can listen to the call and hear first hand how they handled the customer.

- The recording is a tangible link between performance and supervisor feedback. It helps agents clearly identify what skills need improvement. In turn, the supervisor coaches the agent for performance improvement.

- Recorders can be programmed to monitor an agent during set periods of time. This frees up supervisors and provides them with more flexibility and control.

- "Dead time," the period of time a supervisor waits for calls to arrive (as experienced with the silent monitoring method) is eliminated.

Drawbacks

- Providing immediate feedback can be a challenge. Due to supervisors' busy schedules, agents may receive feedback so long after the fact that the window of learning has closed.
- The randomness of this approach makes it a challenge to find calls that provide "coaching opportunities." Those calls that should be used as learning opportunities could quite easily be overlooked. In a nutshell, this approach, like others that rely on random screening, is not intentional and focused enough to result in a strong correlation between quality monitoring and coaching and improved agent performance.
- Not all companies have the storage capacity necessary to contain a sizeable volume of recorded calls. (It bears noting that this phenomenon is becoming less of an issue as storage costs continue to drop.)

Voices and Screens Recorded, Monitored Later

The world-class companies that participated in this study record all transactions. The best systems capture voice, screen and ACD activity for all phone contacts, chat transcripts with timing for Web chats, and e-mail transcripts with timing on e-mail interactions. Capturing the holistic view of the contact provides a complete picture of the customer's experience. The length of time these companies retain their recordings varies.

Recommended Best Practices: Create a Quality Combination

A combination of call recording, and side-by-side monitoring provides the foundation for a successful quality-monitoring program. Each method provides unique benefits that, when coordinated effectively, enable supervisors to give agents well-rounded feedback.

The recommended best practice is to record ALL calls, including voices and screens. Then intentionally select from this rich and extensive database those calls that have the highest potential for agent learning through coaching opportunities. This approach usually precludes a random selection, as many calls do not have coaching opportunities.

The most productive approach to call selection in the world-class companies was to program their software system to select only those calls that had some kind of noteworthy aberration, such as the following:

1. The agent talk time was double the average agent's talk time

2. The number of transfers exceeded two

3. The dead air time was over one minute in length

4. The volume of caller and agent voices was such that it indicated disagreement, even anger

Output of the Monitoring Phase

The call centers we observed in this study utilized the output of the monitoring phase in a variety of ways:

A Scoring Data Sheet

The typical output of a monitoring session is a simple scoring data sheet. Predetermined characteristics of the call are weighted, observed, rated, and scored.

Specific List of Skill Deficiencies

A slight addition to the basic score sheet includes a listing of skill deficits that need correcting.

Training Recommendations

A further improvement to just listing the skill deficits is to include specific training recommendations for each skill deficit.

Tracked Coaching Tips

Some centers also track the areas coached so that future evaluations can look for specific behavior changes based on the prior coaching.

Recommended Best Practices

Providing a printed sheet with feedback on each category works best. Less is better, but specific is good. Be careful not to overwhelm the agent with too much information. Information overload causes the agent to shut down; this is exactly what you don't want to happen. Also, some companies become so focused on rating the call on a micro level (i.e., Did the agent say the script without missing a word? Did the agent misspell anything in her internal documentation?), that they miss the bigger picture, namely: *What did the customer think?* World-class call centers kept this key metric as their primary focus.

Which Calls Should be Monitored

Assuming that your company is on board with our recommendation to record all calls, the next decision becomes: Which calls should we monitor and choose for coaching purposes?

Random Selection of Calls

Currently, the most common corporate response to this question is to select calls at random in the hopes of finding calls worth monitoring. Based on our research, this approach is woefully inadequate. The randomness of this method does not provide an accurate reflection of whether or not your agent is consistently delighting your customers. Nor is this approach intentional enough to result in identifying significant coaching opportunities. This approach does not result in a statistically valid measure of the agent's ability or lack thereof.

Calls Selected by the Agent

Getting agents involved in choosing which calls to monitor is an option. Assuming you have a recording system in place, it is relatively easy for the agent to locate calls that definitely delighted the customer. It is as easy for the agent to locate those calls that did not result in customer delight. Listening to calls at both ends of the spectrum provides agents with a fairly representative picture of their skills, as well as their needs for improvement.

Calls Driven by Caller Satisfaction Feedback

Another approach is to start with any caller satisfaction survey information received, assuming the surveys are collected within 24 hours of the call. The call evaluation can be done on those calls and the front-line agent can learn from the actual customer response to the service provided.

The new emerging model promotes starting with direct customer feedback and having the front-line agent's performance rating be determined by the customers themselves.

This eliminates the formal internal evaluation that tries to assess the value the customer would have assigned to the contact because now the customer provides that feedback directly. In the new model, the QA quality monitoring function can be reduced to a sample audit to determine whether internal procedures are being following for those front-line agents that do not receive a significant volume of dissatisfied surveys, which would be audited at the same time they are reviewed.

> **Note:** It is critical that each survey received as a 'dissatisfied' is reviewed to assess whether or not the reason for dissatisfaction was within the front-line agent's control. For situations such as policy or system-related issues, the front-line agent should be 'held harmless.'

Calls Driven by Call Handling Characteristics

In our study, we found that the best call monitoring systems provided exception reporting to identify potential problem areas. The system can be programmed to identify any performance metric that is outside the norm and/or unacceptable. Potential problems identified included:

- **Repeat contacts by customers**. The system can identify how many times the customer has called in the last 30 days. The assumption is the more often a customer has to call in, the more frustrated they are.

- **Hold times**. The system can highlight when the caller is put on hold, the length of each hold time, and the total hold time per call. A supervisor may choose to review interactions where the customer was put on hold three or more times. The supervisor recognizes the high probability that the front-line agent has a knowledge gap or needs some help in knowing how to effectively handle that particular call-type.

- **Voice Variance**. The system can flag calls where voices escalate and/or talk over one another.

- **Application Driven**. The system can be programmed to look for any performance metric that is out of line. This includes metrics like talk time, after call work time, hold time, transfers, or extended dead air time.

Recommended Best Practices

- ***Cases Selected Based on Coaching Opportunity:*** In the traditional setting, when front-line agent development is the focus, the best practice is to select "outlier" calls, where there is a higher likelihood for coaching opportunities. For example, reviewing contacts where the customer was put on hold three or more times. There is a high probability that the front-line agent has a knowledge gap or needs some help in knowing how to effectively handle that particular call type. This approach only works when the front-line agent's performance evaluation is based on customer satisfaction and not on contact evaluation scores.

- ***Customer-Driven Quality Monitoring:*** In the emerging model, the customer determines the rating of the service experience. The quality assurance team is redeployed as a Trigger Team, who coach front-line agents on cases when the customer has expressed their dissatisfaction with the service provided (see figure 58).

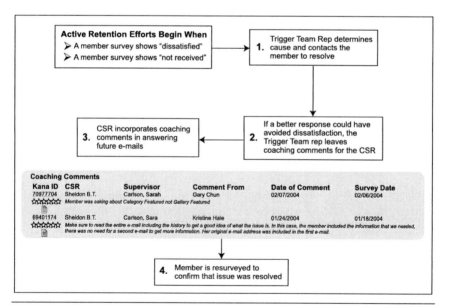

Figure 58. Quality Monitoring Customer Retention Model

What is Measured During Monitoring

Telephone Techniques and Etiquette

This is the most common area for quality monitoring and can be done by individuals not steeped in product details. In this area, the person reviewing the call is placing him/herself in the role of the customer and assessing the effectiveness of the service provided. Although direct customer feedback is most ideal, when the customer is not providing the direct feedback on effectiveness, anyone with good service judgment skill can provide this type of evaluation.

Product Knowledge

Most companies continue to view *accuracy of the answer provided* as the most essential purpose of quality monitoring. Often the bulk of the final score of the call is based on this need for accuracy. While no one would diminish the essentialness of accurate answers, we believe this should be only part of the final evaluation. The customer experience is also essential.

System Efficiency/Screen Navigation

This is a relatively new area. Now that screen navigation can be recorded along with the voice component, the person monitoring the call can determine the effectiveness of the agent's skill in navigating the system to resolve inquiries. To deliver a quality call in an efficient period of time, screen navigation skills are essential. Monitoring this area can result in a wealth of opportunities to coach on short cuts and efficiency skills.

Company Policies and Procedures

Companies naturally have policies that agents are taught and that must be followed. Quality monitoring is a perfect time to see if these policies are adhered to during the call. These policies could be related to warranty limitations, risk management issues, and complaint documentation.

Potential Fraud Issues

Order taking call centers can be vulnerable to fraud related issues. An example is when an agent is pressured to make certain sales goals. The agent signs up a customer for a special when, in fact, the caller explicitly declined the up-sell. The phone companies even have a word for this practice, namely "cramming."

Recommended Best Practices

This is where there emerges a divergence of philosophy. There are two schools of thought. The best traditional thinking is that the criteria for success in call evaluations focuses on how effectively front-line agents resolve customer issues, on how well agents demonstrate professionalism, courtesy and respect for the customer during the call. The potential flaw with this model is that it is still based on an internal view of what someone else "thinks" the customer values.

The new emerging model is when the *customer* actually provides the service assessment of the call. Through surveys, the customer can provide feedback specifically to the agent about what aspects he/she liked or didn't like. The aspects to measure are the attributes that have a direct correlation to the overall satisfaction of the customer.

In the new model, the internal evaluation process incorporates reviewing "failed" service experiences, per the customer (i.e., dissatisfied survey responses) and providing direct coaching to the specific situation.

In the new model, the criteria depends on the reason for the initial contact. For example, if the customer contacted a company about a registration issue, the customer might be asked to evaluate whether the agent seemed sincere in their desire to resolve the issue. Another question might be whether or not the issue was resolved with the information provided.

For the traditional approach, using internally developed criteria, there are several categories that represent the approach most used:

- ***Telephone etiquette***—including opening and closing the call, tone, courtesy and language

- ***Customer interaction and relationship building***—including acknowledgement skills, active listening, articulation skills

- ***Knowledge and information***—including knowledge of product/company, accurate resolution of issue, collects necessary customer information, effective use of resources

- ***Efficiency***—manages the call; solid judgment

- ***Accuracy***—all-important criteria is that the answers must be accurate

Frequency of Agent Monitoring

In our research, we discovered that most call centers typically made it their goal to monitor five calls per agent per month. If we can assume that the average agent handled 1,000+ calls per month, we find that this metric is not quantitatively valid. Even if these organizations monitored double the typical goal of five, their efforts would only result in a 5% confidence level. This means that the probability of choosing a fair representation of calls is only 1 in 20.

Using the 1,000+ calls per agent per month assumption just mentioned, call centers would have to monitor 350 calls per agent every month to reach a 95% confidence level! We have yet to benchmark a call center that can devote the time and resources required to ensure this kind of statistical reliability.

(It bears mentioning that in one of our surveys, we asked call center supervisors to identify their greatest challenges in call monitoring. By far, the greatest challenge identified was *lack of time*.)

Our acknowledgement of the improbability of monitoring 350 calls per agent per month is at the heart of what drove us to find the best practice in this arena. We knew that there was a better way to ensure that quality monitoring was more strongly correlated to increasingly higher levels of customer satisfaction. That better way is the new model that we'll speak to further in the report. It does not require 350 monitored calls per agent per month, but instead relies on an intentional focus to align priority metrics with the customer's perception of their service experience and a redeployment of supervisors.

Frequency of Monitoring New Hires and Those on Probation

The issue of monitoring frequency must take into account not only those agents who are fully functioning but those new hires and exceptions, too.

During First Month Following Release from Class

This is a critical period for a new agent. The best practice is to move the agent from the formal classroom setting to a transitionary "hub" environment. The entire class moves together, and new agents are provided extensive support and coaching during this period. By helping each new agent become confident and competent in their new role, their productivity and quality scores increase quickly. This method shortens the learning curve significantly and helps ensure agent retention during the most stressful stage of their call center career.

During First Six Month of Employment

The new agent still needs more direct attention from their direct supervisor than those who are fully functioning. This is a period when habits form and most agents are very motivated to make a good impression. Mold them with frequent monitoring and coaching while they are still not set in their ways.

After First Six Month of Employment

While all agents should have periodical audits of their work, the highest performing agents can be monitored and coached less if they have proven that they are consistently effective. It's also important to note the particular preferences of each agent. If an agent really thrives on regular positive feedback, then continue to monitor and coach as usual. For those that appreciate being recognized for needing less coaching, then a reduced monitoring schedule works well for them.

When Put On Probation

How frequently an organization monitors those on probation depends on the reason for probation. Most world-class companies have developed zero tolerance policies. So, in cases of blatant disservice (i.e., intentionally disconnecting or arguing with a customer), the agent is likely to be formally terminated without a performance plan. If there is no willful intent to provide poor service, then dedicating some additional time and attention may be time well spent.

Agent behavior needs to be monitored closely to either reinforce movement in the right direction or to redirect at first sign of wrong behavior.

Recommended Best Practices

The recommend best practices regarding monitoring frequency in the categories discussed above are as follows:

- ***During the first month following completion of initial training***. The best practice during this period was to monitor and coach the new agent at least two calls per day while in the "safe hub" environment.

- ***During the first six months following release from the safe hub environment***. The best practice during this period was to monitor and coach the agent at least two calls per week.

- ***After approximately the first seven months of employment, or when the agent has reached "solo" status***. The best practice for an experienced agent is to monitor and coach as needed, i.e., to make the experience more customized to each agent's needs. During this period monitoring and coaching may be by exception only, or as dictated by caller dissatisfaction feedback, or unusual performance metrics. For instance, long average handle times, above average "dead air" time during the phone call, and the like.

- ***Should the agent be placed on probation for any reason?*** If an agent is on probation, the best practice is to monitor and coach the agent at least three times per week. These sessions need to be documented in greater detail than normal agent interactions.

Who Does the Monitoring

There are several models developed around who actually performs the quality assessments. This section addresses these models and points out which ones are most conducive to exceptional call quality monitoring and coaching.

A Dedicated Quality Team

One of the most popular models is a dedicated team whose primary responsibility is to monitor 5-10 contacts for each front-line agent each month. The purpose of the observations is to identify skill gaps. The team provides constructive suggestions to improve the service levels. The majority of those operating in this model use evaluation criteria which attempts to assess the service experience from the assessor's perspective. Evaluations may or may not be tied to the performance assessment process.

The Direct Supervisor

Another most common model assigns front-line supervisor responsibility for monitoring some or all of the agent calls. This was especially true when most supervisors were selected from the agent ranks and had call handling experience in the center.

Peer Monitoring

A third approach, not as common as the prior two, is where a team of product experts monitors lesser-experienced agents.

A Third-party Outsourced Company

Another alternative is to outsource the monitoring process. Companies now exist that will accept the recorded voices, and do the monitoring and scoring process. The end product is a scoring sheet on every call along with corrective actions the coach can suggest to the agent.

Recommended Best Practices

A combination approach works best. Having a dedicated quality team provides the framework to ensure that the evaluations are performed each month. The coaching, however, should be done by the direct supervisor. The supervisor needs to be dedicated to team development rather than outside activities. The supervisor also needs to be credible by having current knowledge about the position and the subjects handled.

Who Should do the Coaching

A major problem encountered during our study was that supervisors simply did not have the time to coach based on monitored results. In fact, in a study fielded to all of our community members, we found the time crunch to be a key obstacle.

A Team of Coaching Experts

Often in a center handling very complex calls, only real experts can truly evaluate the level of the agent's understanding of the question or issue. In such a situation, it may be mandatory that product specialists be assigned to monitoring.

The Direct Supervisor

The direct supervisor is the most common and most logical agent coach.

A Third-party Outsourced Company

Because of the tremendous time burden of coaching, often there is simply not enough time in the day to do this activity completely by the internal staff. A number of third-party outsourcing companies have sprung up to assist. When properly trained, they can do a very professional job.

Recommended Best Practices

Front-line management should be dedicated to agent development

The role of front-line supervisors is to develop the talents of their teams. They own the performance of their team, including the satisfaction level of the callers that they serve. We observed that majority of world-class supervisors spent their time in:

- side-by-side coaching with the front-line team members
- reinforcing right behaviors and coaching others
- removing obstructions to providing world-class service
- communicating performance results/trends
- co-developing development plans with front-line team members
- sharing and learning best practices with co-leadership
- sharing best practices within the team
- creating/maintaining positive environment—team building
- handling irate situations, modeling approach for learning

More than 90% of the supervisor time should be spent with and among the team. World-class companies recognize that they have the most pivotal role in determining the success and performance level of the front-line team. They are not pulled away for project work or corporate initiatives.

Ratio of supervisors to front-line agents is important

The front-line supervisor has 13-15 team members as direct reports. There is a commitment to keep the ratio within this range. Newer front-line supervisors may have fewer as they learn how to be an effective people-developer.

Supervisors hired for leadership skills

Rather than promoting the best technical employee, world-class companies understand that, while content knowledge is important, that knowledge can be trained. It is more important to ensure the right person is in this role than any other role in the contact center. Ideal is hiring agents who have shown, through aptitude testing and prior history, that they have the ability to excel as a leader.

Training for supervisor role

World-class companies invest in their leaders. Because the success of the center is based on the performance of the front-line team, and the front-line leaders are responsible for developing their team, they need to be well trained for the position. They are trained in the leadership philosophy of the organization; in best practices in motivating and sharing feedback; in team building and on how to read and interpret the reporting for their team and the center. They are also involved in ongoing training to continually improve their leadership effectiveness.

> **Note:** It is important that no matter who does the coaching, that the coach understands the essentialness of agent "self-discovery." It is critical that the coach doesn't force feed the agent his or her evaluations but guides the agent to self-discovery through strategically asked questions.

Sharing Monitoring Results with the Agent

We have discovered a variety of ways that the monitoring results are shared with the individual agent.

By E-mail

One method was to have the supervisor's score sheet sent to the agent by e-mail. The agent is then taught to do a level of self-coaching by reviewing the feedback and, in some cases, respond with planned actions to improve performance. This is not ideal.

By Personal Feedback Coach

A feedback coach meets with each agent and reviews the results. They then share the evaluations with the agent's direct supervisor.

By the Direct Supervisor

The direct supervisor reviews the monitored results. The supervisor is also responsible for the performance of the team and the behaviors of each front-line agent. The supervisor, therefore, is essential in facilitating the learning of each front-line agent in the areas needed.

Recommended Best Practices

Build an environment of trust to open the possibilities for change

Front-line agents feel supported and encouraged in world-class companies. Everyone from senior leadership to the classroom trainers is dedicated to the agent's success.

Remember that self-discovery is key

World-class companies know that no one changes until they decide to change. This is a key differentiator between world-class companies and those that are not yet world-class. World-class leaders know how to share the feedback. Whether the feedback is from the customer directly or from the quality internal evaluation, the supervisor will ask questions that lead the agent to self-discovery.

Keep in mind that words do matter

The actual <u>words</u> chosen for coaching have a significant impact on whether or not the agent 'hears' the message. Unless a person agrees that a behavior needs to be changed, the most that will happen is forced compliance. One world-class company specifically opens the feedback sessions with the question:

> "After listening to the call, would there be anything you would change?"

Rather than ask "what would you change" which implies that there was something that needed to be changed, the words chosen make "nothing" a viable answer. An old adage may apply here: *A man forced to change opinion under will is of the same opinion still.*

Personalizing the message is best

Since much of behavior modification is driven from an agent's decision to make a change, the direct supervisor needs to know each front-line agent individually. Each agent is wired differently.

And the better the supervisor understands the agent's values and what motivates them, the better that supervisor's chance is to influence and impact the agent's performance. In the same way that agents are trained to adjust their style to meet each customer's needs, the supervisor must adjust their leadership style to meet each agent's professional needs.

Timing is definitely critical

Results from customer surveys should be reviewed with the front-line agent within 24-hours of the call. Feedback beyond that point loses impact and credibility.

Tracking areas for improvement is essential

A best practice is to track the areas that the front-line agent is focused on improving and look for improvement in those specific areas on the next evaluations. Changing behavior is not easy. Reinforcing the right behaviors by recognizing improved results increases the chance for continued agent success.

Who does the feedback can be key. Our study revealed two models:

1. The monitor who conducted the evaluation provided the feedback for those calls scored

2. The monitor forwards the feedback to the direct supervisor, who reviews it with the front-line agent

If the other aspects are present (i.e., supportive environment, those giving feedback are well trained, metrics focused on customer satisfaction, etc.), either model works. But no matter which option works for your call center, ensure your supervisors monitor and provide feedback to each agent at least once per month to stay involved.

Listening to calls is important

A best practice is to include self-assessment of calls as a normal part of the agent development process. Having agents actually listen to the calls and score themselves on their performance is one of the most powerful behavior improvement techniques available. Agents can "hear" their weaknesses when they listen to the call, especially if trained to do so by professional coaching.

At one company we benchmarked, the agents actually listen to eight calls per month and submit the five best for formal evaluation. Another company has *Perfect Call Contests*. Agents can submit any call they feel was perfect for consideration.

Compensation Impact

Pay for Performance

Monitoring systems are often tied to performance pay. Using a traditional model, there is not enough sample size to statistically support using the numbers for performance assessments.

Reward and Recognition

It is quite common to tie rewards and recognition to monitoring systems. There are many effective versions of tying reward and recognition to the "right behaviors." The most effective methods allow for customization of the rewards to each agent's personal preferences.

Recommended Best Practices

World-class call centers typically combine both practices. When tying pay to performance, it is essential that agents receive short-term incentives, such as monthly goals tied to pay outs based on their ability to delight the customer. Compensation programs that pay agents strictly based on longevity or for their acquisition of a specific skill set have their limitations. The caution with both is that they fail to recognize that an organization may end up paying money for a complacent veteran and/or for a skilled, but unmotivated agent.

Key Performance Indicators

The following addresses the key performance indicators that should be used in the call quality monitoring process.

Agent Expectations Tied to Customer Satisfiers

Performance expectations for agents and supervisors should reflect a commitment to delighting the customer. Expectations are tied to key customer satisfiers and clearly communicate the extent to which agents are empowered to serve customers. Mixed messages are avoided (e.g., agents are told to take the time needed to satisfy callers and, hence, should not be directly evaluated on the average length of the calls they handle).

Connecting Internal Metrics to External Measurements

Figure 59. Overall center metrics focused on customer

Predicting quantitative and qualitative measures for achieving customer satisfaction is a necessary place to start. However, actual customer satisfaction rates, as indicated by the customer, are the central focus. Productivity and efficiency measures are focused on effective use of staff, technology, and employee satisfaction. (Most world-class call centers recognize that employee satisfaction is a primary predictor of productivity and efficiency.) Measures are continuously compared to industry data, including industry average, best competitor, and appropriate benchmarks.

Management Information

Front-line managers review statistics on calls, such as numbers of calls, ASA, service level, call lengths, after call work time, and other measures for their group or individual front-line team members. These are used to help improve overall performance and staffing levels, not to criticize the agents. Managers review exception reports for individual-based metrics, such as talk time, average hold time, and after call work as indicators of possible problems areas for coaching.

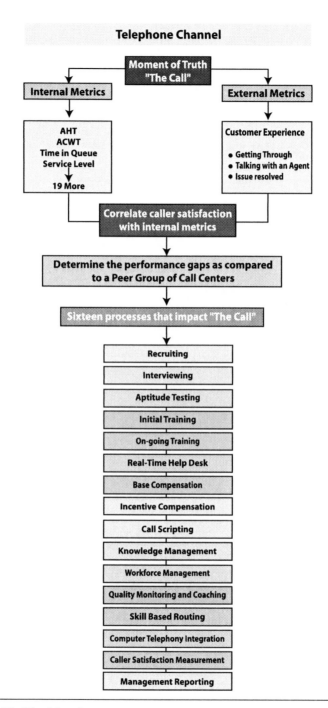

Figure 60. The big picture

Recommended Best Practices

World-class companies evaluate contacts based on direct indicators that drive customer satisfaction. By analyzing the results from their customers, they determine what internal metrics are representative of the customers' perception of the service experience.

In the evolving model, the customer determines the criteria to assess the service level. Starting with universal service metrics, such as resolved on 1st contact and easy accessibility, World-class companies ask their customers to determine how well the front-line agent performed. Based on the suggestions to improve the service experience, World-class companies evolve the questions to provide actionable feedback on what the customer deems most important. The role of the internal review then changes to an auditing role.

Key Performance Indicators for Quality of Calls Handled

- % top box score on overall customer satisfaction (rated 5 out of 5 or 10 out of 10 by the customer)
- % resolved on first contact (as rated by the customer)
- % of accuracy audits that pass

Key Performance Indicators for Quantity of Calls Handled

- adherence to schedule
- occupancy or availability

Other Performance Indicators to Monitor (not always within agent control - Indicator Types) (not absolute list):

- abandon rate
- average speed of answer (ASA)
- average talk time
- average after call work time
- percent of calls transferred

Additional Impact Factors

The following outline lists the factors that have also contributed to the success of the world-class companies in their agent monitoring and coaching process.

Companies that want to significantly improve the results from their agent monitoring and coaching can use this list as a framework:

1. Create the environment where agents are highly valued and respected. Make their satisfaction a priority. Starts with top leadership. Best foundation is "Servant Leadership" principles.

2. Understand that all learning is through "self-discovery."

3. Hire right. Make it "mean something" to work there. Having an effective screening/testing process increases the odds of success both for the agent and the company. Look for aptitudes that embrace change and individuals who are "lifelong learners."

4. Train them well. Bite size, then success...repeat. Based on Situational Leadership model of developing confidence and competence.

5. Provide safety net moving into the real world. The training hub sends the message that the company truly cares about their success.

6. Provide instant access to resources. Expert help desk. Also, track contact reasons for continual process improvement.

7. Define clear expectations. What does success look like? How much latitude do the agents have? With more experience and proven judgment, do they earn more trust and latitude?

8. Use the RIGHT metrics!! "What gets measured, gets done." Focus on first order metrics. Why do we really have a customer service department in the first place? Effectively resolve any questions/concerns in a way that builds loyalty and has a positive "brand" impression.

9. First order metrics:

    • % Top box satisfaction (as measured by the CUSTOMER)

    • % Resolved on 1st contact (as measured by the CUSTOMER)

    • % of contacts passing audit criteria—providing the right answer and not violating any "red rule" company policies

10. Those should be the only measures that tie to performance. Any others should simply be internal gauges to determine the effectiveness of the overall system (i.e., enough resources, call routing, etc.). Examples of these: % of calls transferred, hold times, average speed of answer, abandon rate.

11. Invest in the right technology. Ideal is one that captures voice, screen and ACD data. The more information you have, the more insights you'll have on what created the service experience. Also, allows for more specific call selections.

12. Record everything. Creates the mindset that company takes service seriously and provides high impact information for improvement.

13. Staff to Peaks and Manage Down. This is key. Having enough resources to be able to pull agents from the phone to learn/grow. Using the Covey quadrant, the majority of their time is in the Important/Urgent quadrant. Any sort of learning is in the Important, but Not Urgent quadrant. It will be time well spent.

14. Use BNTO (Business Need Time Off) to manage overstaffing. Works well every time. Many more benefits than making sure there is adequate staffing.

15. Dedicate front-line leadership to agent development. The majority of their role (95+%) should be spent developing the talent on their team. Select the right individuals for this critical role! Their approach can make or break the success of the coaching process.

16. Ensure that front-line leadership is considered expert in the job and typical customer subjects. Credibility factor is huge. Have them on phones 8 hours/month. Reduces the "position power" separation and builds camaraderie.

17. Determine what the core competencies are for the position.

18. Co-evaluate each team member against the core competency criteria.

19. Provide multiple opportunities for self-discovery. Cannot be emphasized enough.

20. Determine why any agent is not performing the desired way (i.e., "15 reasons employees don't do what they're supposed to do").

21. Provide examples of excellent service when gap is "don't know what it looks like...."

22. Understand that in many cases, agents "don't know what they don't know" (i.e., unconsciously incompetent).

23. Have front-line supervisors need to "know" each person on the team. Time spent building rapport, understanding the motivational drivers for each person.

24. Make employee satisfaction a significant success factor for all leadership. This means supervisor satisfaction is factor for managers, etc.

25. Use the "Seven Questions" as a method for measuring climate on monthly basis.

26. Have effective communication systems. As a foundation, use Upward Communication Meetings and ECHO system (every contact has opportunities).

27. Find coaching opportunities through "failed" service experiences (as defined by the CUSTOMER). When customers indicate "dissatisfaction" then determine whether within agent's control. If yes, review case with agent and co-discovery opportunities for improvement.

28. Audit the cases that are flagged as dissatisfied for accurate process/procedures.

29. Conduct supplemental "spot audits" for agents with little/no dissatisfied cases to ensure consistency.

30. Provide agent-specific reward and recognition programs that a) rewards top performers, b) encourages developing agents, and c) discourages slackers.

31. Reinforce the Coaching Environment. When agents self-select cases to be coached on and ask for advice on how to improve, you'll know it's working.

32. Track progress and celebrate success! Make environment one where it's fun to work, fun to learn, and where working there means you're one of the best.

The Emerging Model for Quality Monitoring and Coaching

As stated early in this book, following the best practices described here is a great start down the path of differentiating yourself from your competitor. However, findings from our study also helped us shape an emerging model for quality monitoring and coaching. We are excited to share this information with you.

This new model addresses many of the pitfalls addressed previously. Some of those include: there's not enough data to statistically measure an agent's performance; there's not enough time to perform quality monitoring; and the people doing the monitoring must try to evaluate the level of customer satisfaction. How do you know what really makes your customers happy?

The emerging model for quality monitoring acknowledges that, to be effective, we must recognize that customer service is both an art and a science. As such, it must be measured this way. The "artsy" measurement of the *service experience* acknowledges the essentialness of capturing the customers' perception of their service experience. As we've discussed, today, most organizations try to measure agent performance based on what some level of leadership imagines to be the customers' expectations. The potential flaw with this model is that the criteria are based on an internal view of what someone else thinks the customer values. Obviously, no one is better suited to give this kind of feedback than each individual customer. This truth acknowledges that one customer's definition of delightful service is quite likely different than the next one's.

The "scientific" measurement considers the **accuracy of the audit.** Was the correct answer given? Were the "red rules," those that can never be broken for legal or company reasons, followed? Did the agent display good judgment in some "blue rule" areas? Blue rules are those rules that are established for legitimate reasons but can be bent depending on the situation. Surely, the accuracy of the audit will continue in its importance. Agents may delight their customers but give inaccurate answers to the customers' questions. This is not good service.

Both sides of this model are necessary to building customer loyalty. We are convinced that, while the measurement of audit accuracy will continue in its importance, the trend towards incorporating the customer's voice as the primary half of quality monitoring will gain increasing momentum.

In the emerging model, we actually let the customer assess the call and rate their own satisfaction with the agent. Through surveys, the customer can provide specific feedback regarding what aspects they liked or didn't like. The aspects to measure are the attributes that have a direct correlation to the overall satisfaction of the customer. The customer feedback also helps determine which calls will be monitored.

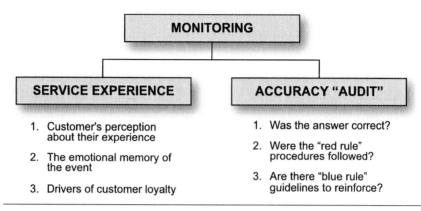

Figure 61. Quality Monitoring and Coaching Model

In the new model, the internal evaluation process incorporates reviewing "failed" service experiences as identified by dissatisfied survey responses. Direct and tailored coaching is then provided to help the agent avoid this issue in the future.

This model uses the customer's view of the **service experience** as the priority focus of the agent's coaching. The secondary focus is the **accuracy audit,** the evaluation of the agent's performance against internal company standards. This approach enables the agent to learn how their service was perceived by the customer, as well as how they met internal quality goals. More importantly, it switches the primary focus from compliance to a mindset of "how can I delight the customer?"

Depending on the customer, delighting the customer may require that the agent be able to establish rapport, build loyalty, or manage the customer's perceptions. The point is to move away from a cookie cutter approach to service excellence and towards the recognition that each customer's needs are unique. The best agents can adapt their behavior to meet the needs of his or her customers.

We see this approach as being not only a best practice, but we endorse it as the central focus of our new vision for quality monitoring and coaching. We cannot emphasize enough the value of utilizing actual customer feedback. This approach eliminates the leaders' need to imagine how the customer would have valued their interaction. The internal guess work is unnecessary because now the customer provides that feedback directly (and, of course, more accurately). The agent is now evaluated based on the degree to which they are able to delight the customer.

This approach is also more cost effective than many other methods of quality monitoring. Instead of using internal resources such as a monitor or supervisor to evaluate countless service experiences, you've put the customers to work as evaluators! So your evaluation results will not only be more accurate, they'll also cost you far less as your customers will evaluate their experience for free.

Agent satisfaction has jumped to the top of the list of concerns for contact center managers, and for good reasons. Research indicates:

1. Happy agents make for satisfied customers; dissatisfied agents drive customers away.

2. Many good ideas come from agents—but you have to ask them.

3. Human resources account for about 60% of total costs in the average center, which means your biggest investment is not in technology, but in your people.

4. Turnover, which averages over 25% for inbound centers globally, is disruptive, causes dissatisfaction among customers and is very expensive. Consider that the average cost of hiring and training a new agent is about $6,500, according to our database.

Consider also that our industry has come from nowhere 30 years ago, and now employs an estimated 3% of the working population in North America. Experts have predicted that this will rise to 5% during this decade. However, our research indicates that wherever the percent of people employed in contact centers exceeds 3.5% in a specified labor zone, competition for people can cause increases in turnover and wage pressures.

The lesson is that paying attention to your agents and making them feel part of something bigger than just a row of computer stations is key to your success. Measuring their satisfaction and gathering their input is important and, properly done, provides a huge ROI. Unfortunately, many companies use the same surveys to measure employee satisfaction across the entire enterprise. We have found that the call center, as a "business within a business," needs its own special employee satisfaction measurement tool.

FairCompare™, an agent satisfaction benchmark product introduced by BenchmarkPortal in 2003 is especially designed to result in actionable information for the call center environment. It gives you the same kind of good, granular inputs that our *Echo*™ product provides for customer satisfaction. It offers a dashboard of hosted reports that help you solve problems <u>before</u> they affect your customer and your turnover. This is an important—and affordable—management tool, which is extremely actionable. Following are some sample screen-shots from the *FairCompare™* reporting module, which shows scores on a key set of metrics.

FairCompare - Results: Your Company

Top & bottom box

This report displays the percentage of responses to top box (i.e. 5 out of 5) and the bottom box (i.e. 1 out of 5) scales. It shows how strongly individuals feel about particular areas. The data is ranked by the top box percentage minus the bottom box percentage.

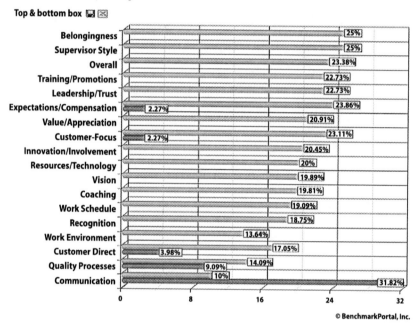

© BenchmarkPortal, Inc.

Figure 62. Example #1 of FairCompare™ Reporting Module

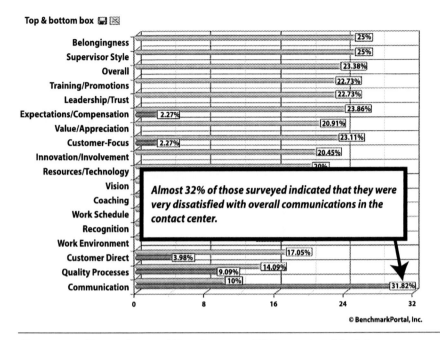

Almost 32% of those surveyed indicated that they were very dissatisfied with overall communications in the contact center.

Figure 63. Example #2 of FairCompare™ Reporting Module

You can also drill down on your results to uncover specific concerns.

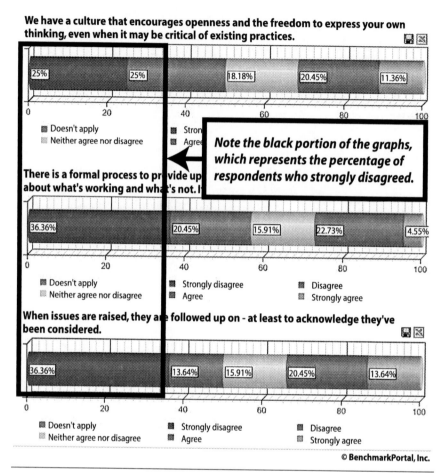

We have a culture that encourages openness and the freedom to express your own thinking, even when it may be critical of existing practices.

Note the black portion of the graphs, which represents the percentage of respondents who strongly disagreed.

There is a formal process to provide up... about what's working and what's not. I...

When issues are raised, they are followed up on - at least to acknowledge they've been considered.

© BenchmarkPortal, Inc.

Figure 64. Example #3 of FairCompare™ Reporting Module

The reporting module is very user friendly, allowing the manager to display, slice or dice the data as they wish. Thus, if you prefer, you can view survey results in a tabular format.

Coaching	0.00%	0.00%	1.95%	18.18%	60.06%	19.81%	100%
Q#	N/A	Strongly Disagree	Disagree	Neutral	Agree	Strongly Agree	Total
1	The coaching process here is formalized...it's not haphazard.	0.00%	0.00%	2.27%	11.36%	63.64%	22.73%	100%
2	I receive feedback on my performance on a regular basis.	0.00%	0.00%	2.27%	22.73%	50.00%	25.00%	100%
3	The coaching I receive helps me improve the service I provide.	0.00%	0.00%	2.27%	27.27%	54.55%	15.91%	100%
4	I look forward to my coaching sessions.	0.00%	0.00%	0.00%	9.09%	77.27%	13.64%	100%
5	If I disagree with an evaluation on my performance, there is an effective appeal process.	0.00%	0.00%	4.55%	18.18%	65.91%	11.36%	100%
6	I receive feedback on both the positive aspects of my performance as well as areas that need work.							
7	I feel that the individuals) that evaluate my service-performance are credible and respected.							

Note that over 70% of respondents either agreed or strongly agree that the coaching they receive helps them improve the service they provide.

Communication							
Q#	N/A	Strongly Disagree	Disagree	Neutral	Agree	Strongly Agree	Total
1	In this organization, you can talk about sensitive issues...there are no taboos.	0.00%	31.82%	18.18%	6.82%	27.27%	15.91%	100%
2	We have a culture that encourages openness and the freedom to express you own thinking, even when it may be critical of existing practices.	0.00%	25.00%	25.00%	18.18%	20.45%	11.36%	100%

© BenchmarkPortal, Inc.

Figure 65. Example #4 of FairCompare™ Reporting Module

The reporting module also lets you set a "filter" to give you superior analytical capabilities. For example, if you would like to review the results for the training questions by employee tenure, or wish to understand overall satisfaction by length of commute, you can select the specific criteria and get your answer. This can ultimately affect your employee retention and recruiting practices to optimize satisfaction and morale.

FairCompare - Results: Your Company

Create Own Report

This section provides the ability to Slice-and-Dice the results for your center. You can decide which report you'd like to view and then specify the "filter" to use. For example, if you'd like to review the results for the training questions by employee tenure, you can select that specific criteria.

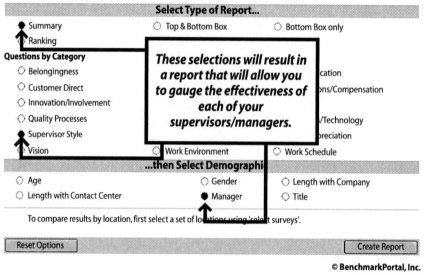

Select Type of Report...

- ● Summary
- ○ Ranking

○ Top & Bottom Box   ○ Bottom Box only

Questions by Category

- ○ Belongingness
- ○ Customer Direct
- ○ Innovation/Involvement
- ○ Quality Processes
- ● Supervisor Style
- ○ Vision

These selections will result in a report that will allow you to gauge the effectiveness of each of your supervisors/managers.

...cation
...ns/Compensation
.../Technology
...reciation

○ Work Environment   ○ Work Schedule

...then Select Demographi

- ○ Age
- ○ Length with Contact Center

○ Gender
● Manager

○ Length with Company
○ Title

To compare results by location, first select a set of locations using 'select surveys'.

Reset Options   Create Report

© BenchmarkPortal, Inc.

Figure 66. Example #5 of FairCompare™ Reporting Module

This information can give you a wealth of insight into improving morale and productivity, and can be used appropriately for planning, recruiting and scheduling purposes as well.

BenchmarkPortal also launched an agent satisfaction benchmarking service that allows you to compare your agent satisfaction with other centers in your industry or geographic area.

CHAPTER 11: PERFORMANCE COMPENSATION—GETTING EVERYONE FOCUSED ON THE MISSION

Background

A practical and efficient performance compensation plan for your contact center team members should have the following characteristics:

1. The process should be simple and cost effective to implement and maintain.

2. The input metrics should be:

   - easily available, inexpensive to collect, input, and process

   - simple to interpret by all involved

   - unquestionable in their accuracy and validity

   - indicative of caller satisfaction and/or cost of doing business

   - directed to the achievement of the mission of your contact center

3. The results should cause little to no debate, disagreement, or protest between executive management and your contact center or team members.

4. The results should be usable not only to encourage certain positive outcomes, but also to penalize negative outcomes.

5. The results should be usable to manage continuous improvement.

The following is a summary outline for a practical and efficient analysis/performance plan for your team members. The plan integrates the key external caller satisfaction metrics with internal operational metrics and is made up of two distinct parts:

1. An incentive/disincentive compensation plan for your team members

2. An ability to identify best practices for continuous improvement initiatives by team leaders working closely with contact center management

The Performance Compensation Plan

Our research shows that there are two high-level metrics that are most indicative of a world-class contact center. Therefore, these two metrics are our choice for driving a performance compensation plan for contact center team members (Anton, 1996). Effectively, a contact center manager should focus on managing a balance between caller satisfaction and cost of achieving caller satisfaction.

The plan should entail rewards for exceeding the standards and would have no penalty when standards were not met; thus it would be a positive reward system. However, below the set performance standards, compensation would be painfully low, thereby discouraging the teams from operating at minimum standards. This point will become clearer in subsequent discussions and examples.

The two most important high-level metrics are:

1. The Caller Satisfaction Index (or CSI), which is created by combining the main indicators of caller delight (overall satisfaction, willingness to continue service, and willingness to recommend).

2. The most comprehensive measure of fiscal containment, which is the actual contact center budget (costs) divided by the number of full-time equivalent (or contact center cost/FTE).

The CSI would be designed to be indicative of the caller's impression of three mission-critical parts of a telephonic moment of truth:

1. The accessibility of the contact center
2. The interaction with the agent
3. The answer/solution provided by the agent

The Cost/FTE would be a calculation of the total costs to operate your contact center divided by the total number of FTEs working during the period of performance measurement. The period may be either a month or a quarter, depending on desired frequency of feedback. We suggest that the CSI scores should never be less than 50 and may reach a maximum of 100. The cost/FTE should range from a minimum of $40,000 to a maximum of $55,000. The matrix shown below is an overview of the performance compensation model.

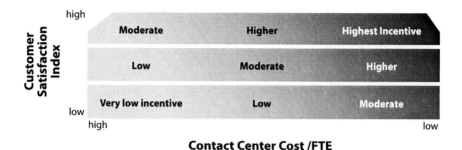

Figure 67. Relating performance to compensation

As a more specific example of implementing the above matrix, we have added percentage compensation increases depending on the overall performance of the contact center. This expanded matrix is shown below.

Customer Satisfaction Index	55	53.2	51.4	49.6	47.8	46	44.2	42.4	40.6	38.8	37
100	10%	11%	12%	13%	14%	15%	16%	17%	18%	19%	20%
95	9%	10%	11%	12%	13%	14%	15%	16%	17%	18%	19%
90	8%	9%	10%	11%	12%	13%	14%	15%	16%	17%	18%
85	7%	8%	9%	10%	11%	12%	13%	14%	15%	16%	17%
80	6%	7%	8%	9%	10%	11%	12%	13%	14%	15%	16%
75	5%	6%	7%	8%	9%	10%	11%	12%	13%	14%	15%
70	4%	5%	6%	7%	8%	9%	10%	11%	12%	13%	14%
65	3%	4%	5%	6%	7%	8%	9%	10%	11%	12%	13%
60	2%	3%	4%	5%	6%	7%	8%	9%	10%	11%	12%
55	1%	2%	3%	4%	5%	6%	7%	8%	9%	10%	11%
50	0%	1%	2%	3%	4%	5%	6%	7%	8%	9%	10%

Contact Center Cost per FTE (in thousands of dollars)

Figure 68. Relationship between performance and compensation

Some notes about the above matrix are in order:

1. The matrix is used to pay a bonus (not impose a penalty) such that you motivate the contact center and the teams to focus on the key measures of success, which are delivery of maximum caller satisfaction at a minimum cost. The inherent disincentive is that the teams would be paid a base rate so low that they will need to excel in the performance measures of CSI and Cost/FTE in order to earn their desired level of compensation.

2. As the teams exceed the standard for each of the measures, the team would receive a corresponding percentage of the contact center's bonus pool.

3. All of the numbers in this chart are arbitrary and are shown only to better explain the concept of the incentive plan. The

management of each contact center would need to tailor the percentages to meet their compensation and performance goals.

Details about the Cost/FTE

It is mission-critical for the Cost/FTE to be composed of data components that are simple and incontestable. The following are some guidelines.

1. The cost should simply be the total of all expenses reported for the time period.

2. This could either be done on a cash accounting basis (i.e., all bills paid during the measurement period) or on an accrual basis (i.e., all invoices received during the period). Once the accounting system is agreed on, there would be few exceptions to what is included and what is excluded.

3. The number of FTEs would come straight from the payroll records for the period.

4. Cost/FTE is the only business measure that includes all other normal contact center metrics. Cost/FTE is directly affected by queue time, percent abandon, talk time, average handle time, transfer percent, hold time, problem resolution costs, number of calls handled, agent turnover rate, average seconds to answer, credits to accounts, etc.

The contact center business has expanded at a near exponential rate during recent years. Increases in the number of callers, calls, and contact centers are changes in the basic structure of the industry itself. The major contact center trends over recent years include:

- Contact center strategy has moved from niche marketing to corporate mission critical capability. In some industries 95% of the business is conducted over the telephone and the Internet.

- Modern technologies are being combined through computer-integrated telephony.

- The cost of agents is a growing percent of the total contact center budget. In the 1990s agent costs were 54% of the contact center budget—now they are more than 70%.

- Senior management is demanding better information from contact center managers to justify the escalating expenses.

With such dramatic changes occurring, it becomes more critical for the operation to be efficient and effective. Technology providers, trainers, and managers have responded with a plethora of solutions to the need for efficiency and effectiveness as now defined by hearing the caller's directions. This new need to be effective as well as efficient can be summed up in the value of a solid contact center management information system. The components of such a system are described below:

- improvement in agent performance through business based performance reporting

- more effective use of training time by better targeting agent needs

- improved VRU utilization through analysis of call flow patterns

- improved caller service through beginning to end call tracking

- customer retention through better feedback on service levels and the nature of inquiries

- company wide information in contact center resource utilization for executive decision-making

A

Abandon Rate: An internal metric of all calls that get connected to the call center but are disconnected by the caller before reaching an agent, outbound trunk, or information announcement. The abandon rate is the percentage of calls that are abandoned compared to calls received.

ACD: Automatic Call Distributor. A device that forwards incoming calls to the next available TSR or answering position.

Adherence to Schedule: A measure of whether agents are "on the job" as scheduled. Adherence is determined by comparing scheduled time when an agent is supposed to be at work, as compared to the actual time an agent is at work. The question, "how often do agents deviate from their schedule" is answered by this metric.

After Call Work Time: This is the time after a call is completed that the agent needs to complete administrative work related to the call. The data for after call work time is taken from the ACD and should be calculated by individual and group, daily, weekly, and monthly.

Agent Turnover: This is the number of agents who left in the course of a year as a percentage of the total number of agents working during that same period. Turnover is calculated by comparing the number of agents who left their "agent job" in the previous year, divided by the average number of agents working during the year and stating this answer as a percentage. The average number of agents is calculated by taking the beginning year agent head count plus the end of year agent head count, and dividing the sum by two.

ANI: Automatic Number Identification. ANI is a service of telecommunications carriers, which identifies the telephone number of the calling party. It is commonly used for billing, call routing and database synchronization. There are several specific technologies that fit under the umbrella of ANI, including caller ID.

Average Attendance in percent: This is a percentage representing how often an agent is NOT absent from work due to an unplanned absence (not to include excused absences, i.e., vacation, FMLA, jury duty, etc.). Take the total number of unexcused absences and divide it by the total number of absenteeism opportunities and subtract that number from 100.

Average Cost per Call: This is the sum of all costs for running the call center for the period divided by the number of calls handled in the call center for the same period. This would include all calls for all reasons whether handled by an agent or technology, such as IVR.

Average Handle Time: An internal metric that is the sum of talk time, hold time, and after call work time.

Average Sale Value per Sale: When agents are taking orders, it becomes important to know the average sale value of individual sales. This number is determined by taking the total sales in dollars during a period of time, let's say a week, and dividing this by the total number of sale calls handled during the same period of time.

Average Speed of Answer (ASA): Equal to the total time in queue divided by the total number of calls answered. This includes both technology-handled calls as well as live agent calls.

Average Talk Time: Total number of seconds the caller was connected to an agent.

Average Time in Queue: The average length of time (in seconds) a caller must spend waiting before the ACD can find an available TSR to take the call. This number is not the equivalent of Average Speed of Answer, as it includes only those calls that actually experience a wait for a live agent. Also known as, "average time of delay."

B

Best-in-Peer Category: This represents the top twenty five percent of the peer group with the best multi-view call center performance index (MPI).

Beta: The slope coefficient of a regression equation.

Bivariate Analysis: Statistical analysis which proceeds by simultaneous analysis of two variables.

Best Practice: Best practice is the best performing metric in a category.

C

Calls per Hour: The average number of calls that an agent handles per hour, and is equal to the total calls handled during a working shift, divided by the total time (in hours) logged into the telephone system.

Confidence Interval: The range around a numeric value obtained from a sample, within which the actual, corresponding value for the population is likely to fall, at a given level of probability.

Cost per Call: This is the sum of all costs for running the call center for the period, divided by the number of calls handled in the call center for the same period. This would include all calls for all reasons whether handled by an agent or technology, such as IVR. You can also just calculate the cost per call for agent-handled calls. The number of calls received will be captured by the ACD. The total cost of the center can be obtained from your accounting department.

Cross-Sell: A cross-sell occurs when an agent recognizes that the caller might be able to use a product from the same company, but in a totally different product line within the company. For instance, an agent at a banking call center who is opening a savings account for a caller might recognize the advantage for the caller to purchase a CD from the bank at a higher interest rate.

CTI: Computer-Telephony Integration refers to the linkage of a telephone switch (ACD, PBX) and computer systems to enhance call processing. Common applications include screen pop, simultaneous voice and data transfer, and IVR.

Customer Access Channels: Customer access channels are the multiple ways that customers can reach out and contact a company. A few of the obvious access channels are telephone, e-mail, fax, normal mail, kiosk, and face-to-face.

Customer Centric: Placing the wants and needs of the customer as the central focus of all business practices within the firm. Seeing your business through the, "eyes of the customer."

Customer Lifetime Value: The imputed dollar revenues or profits (depending on formula) generated by the customer for as long as the customer remains with the firm.

Customer Retention: Keeping a customer as opposed to losing the customer to the competition. A percentage of this figure would be the tenure of the average customer with the firm as computed by the sum of the time of all customers with the firm, divided by the number of customers.

Customer Satisfaction: This is a state of mind that a customer has about a company in which their expectations have been met or exceeded over the lifetime of the product. This leads to company loyalty and product repurchase.

Customer Share: The percent of those who purchase the item of interest from a given firm. Computed as the number of customers who purchase the item from a given firm, divided by the number of customers who purchase the item from all firms combined.

Customer Value Segment: Customer value segmentation strives to segment customers based on their financial value to the company. This value is usually based on a combination of the total amount of money that a customer spends with the company, and the profitability of that revenue stream. The best example would be the frequent flyer programs that the airlines have. United, for instance, has the following value segments with its frequent flyer program: a) regular frequent flyer, b) premium frequent flyer, and c) 1K frequent flyer.

D

Data Mining: Data mining refers to the actual process of analyzing the data in a data warehouse. The data miner decides what queries are required of the database, and uses a special query language to create the reports.

Data Warehousing: Data warehousing refers to the logical and strategic ordering and storage of contact data into a database thereby allowing easy and intuitive analysis and reporting. This generally requires a company to connect multiple, existing databases.

Dependent Variable: This is the variable, which is to be predicted from the independent variable(s). For example, if "satisfaction with talk time" were the dependent variable, then "talk time" would be the independent variable from which satisfaction could be predicted.

DNIS: Dialed Number Identification Service. A carrier service for 800/888 and 900 numbers that forwards the number dialed by the caller to the called party.

E

Efficiency Index: The index is calculated by statistically combining into an index those metrics that are indicative of efficient performance. This is considered to be productivity and focuses on the cost of operating the business.

Effectiveness Index: The index is calculated by statistically combining into an index those metrics that are indicative of effective performance. This is considered to be quality and is impacted by customer-focused processes.

External Metrics: These are usually characterized as "soft" numbers as they are the collected attitudes, opinions, and emotions of customers or other interested parties. The data may be collected by survey, focus group, or interview methods. This represents the customer perspective.

F

Focus Group: A personal, simultaneous interview among a small group of individuals. It depends more on group discussion than individual responses for the data generated.

H

Help Desk: The term typically applied to an "internal" call center that handles primarily calls from employees about technical problems with their computer, monitor, printer, and the like.

Hold Time: This is the average number of seconds that an agent places customers on hold during a call. Most ACDs can provide this number as a total number of hold seconds and then you can compute the average hold time.

I

Independent Variable: An input variable from which the dependent variable can be predicted. For example, if "satisfaction with talk time" were the dependent variable, then "talk time" would be the independent variable from which satisfaction could be predicted.

Internal Metrics: These are generated by computers internal to call center technology (PBS, ACD, or VRU) or through departments such as Accounting, Finance, or Human Resources. Internal metrics are commonly perceived as "hard" numbers. Examples include average handle time, queue time, and abandon rate. This is generally not representing the view the customer has of your company.

IVR: Interactive Voice Response. Technology that allows a customer making an inbound call to interact with the data systems by responding to a menu of options. Responses are typically entered by pressing the keys on the telephone keypad; however, voice recognition is becoming more commonly integrated into the process, thus providing a more useful tool.

M

Mean: The most common measure of central tendency, it is computed as the sum of the items divided by the number of items.

Median: The median is the value above and below which one-half of the observations fall.

Moment of Truth: (MOT) is a critical interaction between the customer and the product or service or employee that determines whether the customer will continue to purchase from the vendor.

N

Negative Relationship: Relationship between two variables such that when the value of one variable increases, the value of the second decreases. In a plotted regression equation, the regression line will slope downward as viewed from the point of origin.

O

Average Percent Occupancy Factor: The average percent occupancy is determined by taking the time that an agent is in their seat ready to answer calls as compared to the total number of hours that are at work. Therefore, if an agent is at their desk and ready to answer phone calls 4 hours out of an 8-hour shift, the agent's occupancy is 50%.

Outbound Performance Metrics: These are all the measurements that indicate the performance of an outbound telephone agent. Examples might include calls/agent/shift or sales/agent/shift.

Outsourcing: Contracting with an outside company/vendor to handle some or all of your company's inbound and/or outbound telephone calls or contacts.

Order Taking and Tracking: This is a specific function of customer service and it means that this call center specializes in just taking orders and tracking orders.

P

Peer Group: Peer group does not necessarily connote competitors, but most often are the call centers that have the same profile of activities that you have. For instance, a peer group might be all call centers handling mostly inbound calls that are mostly business-to-business, in a call center of over 100 agents, for a company with annual revenues of over one billion dollars.

Percent Blocked Calls: An internal metric that is the number of callers who received a busy signal and, hence, could not get through to the ACD.

Percent Abandoned: An abandoned call is any call that gets connected to the call center but is disconnected by the caller before reaching an agent, outbound trunk, or information announcement. The abandon rate is the percent of calls that are abandoned compared to all calls actually connected to the ACD. The data for this metric is available from the ACD.

Percent agent Utilization: Agent utilization is the percentage of time that an agent is in their seat ready to handle calls as compared to the actual time they are in telephone mode. Utilization equals the product of average call handle time (talk time + hold time + after call work time) and the average number of inbound calls per agent per 8-hour shift (ACPS), divided by total time the agent is connected to the ACD and ready to handle calls during a shift, i.e., occupancy (not in percent).

$$Utilization = \frac{(ATT + AHT + ACW)(ACPS)}{Occupancy}$$

Percent Attendance: Actual number of shifts worked, divided by the planned number of shifts, times 100.

Percent Calls Handled on the First Call (aka, First Time Final): The percentage of calls that do not require an additional call to the call center, or return calls by the agent in order to resolve the issue in the original call. This allows for transferred callers.

This information is often hard to find or inaccurate. Some clients calculate it based on the coding an agent does at the end of a call. If this is the case, the information will be in the ACD. However, this type of calculation almost certainly overstates the percent, since it only subtracts those callers who an agent is certain will call back later; many callers whose issues have been coded by agents as having been resolved will almost certainly call back later and therefore the number is lower. The best way to calculate first time final is to analyze call data over a period of time. This is made easier if the client has a CIM package.

Percentage of Calls Placed in Queue: An internal metric, which is simply the number of calls placed in the queue divided by the total of all calls received by the center.

Percentage of Calls Transferred: An internal metric that is the percentage of total calls transferred from the original agent to someone else.

Plot: A graphic plot of the data points for two variables so that each data point is plotted horizontally according to the value of the dependent variable.

Population: The definition of all the elements, people, or groups of interest for a given research work. The sample will be drawn from the defined population, and the result of the research will be generated to that population.

Positive Relationship: Relationship between two variables such that when the value of one increases, the value of the second also increases. In a plotted regression, the line will slope upward as viewed from point of origin.

Q

Queue Time: This is the average number of seconds that a caller spends waiting for a TSR to answer the telephone after being placed in the queue by the ACD. This generally is calculated after any announcements are provided to the customer

R

Random Sample: A sampling frame that seeks to ensure that all members of the population have an equal chance of being included in the sample. The method to produce this result is to draw completely without structure or randomly from the population of interest.

Regression: A statistical measure of the effect of one interval or ratio level variable on another, used to indicate the statistical significance of the relationship and to generate an equation to predict or estimate the value of the dependent variable for a new case, based only on the known value of the dependent variable.

Rejection: The customer's state of mind such that disengagement from the current relationship has already been decided and has been or soon will be implemented. Negative word-of-mouth is likely to occur.

Risk Analysis: This uses cross-tab tables in combination with top- or bottom-scale analysis. It concentrates on the relationship between individual attribute satisfaction and some dependent variables such as overall satisfaction, willingness to recommend, or intention to remain a customer.

S

Sample: The number and/or identification of respondents in the population who will be or have been included in the survey.

Sample Frame: A listing that includes all those in the population to be sampled, and excludes all those who are not in the population.

Service level: (calls answered in less that X seconds), divided by (offered calls), times 100.

Soft Data: Information or data (such as opinions and attitudes) not based on numbers such as revenue, units sold, costs, etc.

Standard Deviation: The standard deviation is a measure of the dispersion, or variability of the data. In essence this is the average distance of any data point in the distribution from the arithmetic average.

Statistical Significance: An explicit assumption by the analyst that a relationship revealed in the sample data also exists in the population as a whole, based on the relatively small probability that it would result only from sampling error if it did not exist in the population.

Survey Cycle Time: The period during which the survey is conducted. It includes the data collection period plus report generation time.

T

Talk Time: An internal metric for the total number of seconds the caller was connected to a TSR. For purposes of the survey, we ask for this number in minutes.

Total Calls Offered: An internal metric for all calls presented to the center including blocked, abandoned, and handled. This includes calls handled by technology.

Total Annual Budget: The annual dollar amount allocated for all of the expenses associated with the call center including (but not limited to): telecommunications expense, salaries, incentives, equipment, and supplies.

Touch-point: Touch-point is a "buzzword" for customer access channels.

TSR: Telephone Service Representative. A general term for someone who handles telephone calls in a call center. Other common names for the same job include, but are not limited to: operator, attendant, representative, customer service representative (CSR).

U

Up Sell: To sell a higher value product to an existing customer. For example: to lease a more expensive copier to an existing customer. Also, see Cross Sell.

V

Value Creating Gap: This represents a performance gap where your call center is doing better than your peer group.

Value Destroying Gap: This represents a performance gap where your call center is doing worse than your peer group.

Voice Response Unit (VRU): See IVR.

W

Word-of-mouth (WOM): What a customer hears about a product, service, company, etc., usually from friends or family. Also rumors from unspecified sources.

Wrap Up Time: An internal metric for the time, after a call is completed, that the agent uses to complete administrative work related to the call. Also, called "post call work" and "after call work" time.

Caller Satisfaction Survey Example

The following is a call center survey that has been used to successfully measure external caller satisfaction metrics using an automated voice-response (VRU) computer assisted survey process. You will find much more information about the survey process in Appendix B. The user of this handbook can modify this survey to better-fit specific call center needs while maintaining the structure and function of the original survey.

"Hello, and welcome to _____'s survey. We want to continue to make telephone service improvements based on the feedback we gather from callers like you. We appreciate your willingness to share your opinion of the telephone service you just received."

1. _____ Would you say your question was answered or your problem resolved as a result of this call? Respond by saying "yes" or "no."

For the next several questions, please grade our telephone agent on a 1 to 10 scale with 10 being "the best" and 1 being "the worst."

2. _____ Quickly understood your request.

3. _____ Showed concern when answering your question.

4. _____ Spoke clearly.

5. _____ Had sufficient knowledge about our products and services.

6. _____ Gave a complete answer.

7. _____ Gave you confidence in the solution or answer.

8. _____ Clearly presented your options.

9. _____ Completed your call as quickly as possible.

10. _____ All things considered, on the 1 to 10 scale with 10 being high, how satisfied were you with this call?

11. _____ Because of this interaction with our telephone agent, how likely are you to continue your service?

12. _____ In the future, how likely are you to recommend our company to a friend?

Thank you very much for your time. Your opinions will be helpful in providing the best possible service to you in the future.

E-mail Satisfaction Survey Example

The following is a contact center e-mail survey that has been used to successfully measure external customer satisfaction metrics using an automated e-mail response computer assisted process. You will find much more information about the survey process in Appendix B. The user of this handbook can modify this survey to better-fit specific call center needs while maintaining the structure and function of the original survey.

"Hello, and welcome to _____'s survey. We want to continue to make telephone service improvements based on the feedback we gather from callers like you. We appreciate your willingness to share your opinion of the telephone service you just received."

1. _____ Would you say your question was answered or your problem resolved as a result of this call? Respond by typing "yes" or "no."

For the next several questions, please grade our e-mail agent on a 1 to 10 scale with 10 being "the best" and 1 being "the worst."

2. _____ Completely understood your request.

3. _____ Displayed concern when answering your question.

4. _____ Explained himself/herself clearly.

5. _____ Had sufficient knowledge about our products and services.

6. _____ Provided a complete answer.

7. _____ Gave you confidence in the solution or answer.

8. _____ Clearly presented your options.

9. _____ Responded to your e-mail promptly.

10. _____ All things considered, on the 1 to 10 scale with 10 being high, how satisfied were you with this e-mail contact?

11. _____ Because of this interaction with our e-mail agent, how likely are you to continue your service?

12. _____ In the future, how likely are you to recommend our company to a friend?

Thank you very much for your time. Your opinions will be helpful in providing the best possible service to you in the future.

A widely used option for collecting caller satisfaction data is the use of an automated voice-response or automated e-mail -response system survey process. Immediately upon completion of the contact, a predetermined sample of your customers are automatically transferred to the automated survey system. The automated system plays the survey introduction in a recorded human voice or scripted e-mail and begins asking the survey questions. The system waits for the customer to speak, touch-tone key or type their answer to evaluate each service aspect using a 1-5 or a 1-10 scale. The system essentially operates as if it were a "live-agent" interviewer.

The use of automated survey technology raises a question for contact center managers. How will our customers react to an automated survey? In response to this question, we conducted a test to compare the standard telephone interview methodology with an automated survey system.

Customers to an inbound customer service center were contacted 24 to 72 hours later by an interviewer or immediately after the initial contact by the automated survey system and asked to complete a caller satisfaction survey. In total, 401 customers participated in the survey for a 44% participation rate, compared to 452 callers and a 66% participation rate for the automated survey method.

To further explore customer reaction to the automated survey, we asked customers to rate the acceptability of the survey they had just completed on a scale of 1 to 10 with 1 the lowest. Their responses fell into the categories shown in figure 69.

Customer Rating of Automated Survey

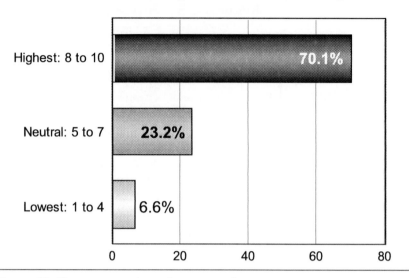

Figure 69. Customer rating of automated survey

Gathering customer perception data using an automated system has several advantages over the more commonly used telephone and mail survey formats:

1. There is considerably less expense per survey.

2. A statistically representative sample at the 95% confidence level can always be collected due to the lower cost per survey.

3. Customer opinions are more accurate because the evaluation occurs immediately or nearly immediately after the initial customer service experience.

4. The customer who experienced the service is always the one to compete the survey.

5. Survey data entry costs are eliminated since the customer enters the data.

6. Errors are significantly reduced if not eliminated altogether.

7. Actual customer comments are recorded verbatim and can be listened to or reviewed and referred to afterwards.

8. Internal metrics can be collected at the same time as the automated survey allowing direct statistical correlation between internal and external metrics.

9. Survey cycle time (period of interest being measured which includes the data collection period + report generation) is considerably shorter.

10. Data can be turned into management information almost immediately.

In figure 70, we present a complete comparison between the automated survey system and the more common mail and telephone survey system.

Characteristics	Automated Survey	Telephone Survey	U.S. Mail Survey
Average time between service experience and evaluation	5 seconds	30 hours	5 days
Average response rate	60%	40%	20%
Data entry errors	low	medium	high
Survey cycle time	7 days	37 days	54 days
Cost per 3 minute survey (numeric data only)	$0.90	$18.00	$5.00
Cost per 3 minute survey (numeric data with 1 open-ended question)	$2.00	$22.00	$7.50

Figure 70. Comparison across survey fielding methodologies

Using automated surveys can reduce your cost and increase the value of your caller satisfaction program. The automated survey system is an exciting tool for quality of service measurement and contact center management.

For more information go to <www.EchoSurvey.com> or contact Lisa Frame at 952.892.5385 or e-mail her at LisaFrame@BenchmarkPortal.com.

APPENDIX C: SAMPLING CONCEPTS

A basic determinant of survey research quality is the proper utilization of a random sample of customers. Random samples permit the use of various statistical techniques to describe and predict the behavior of all customers. The idea is simple: if you draw at random enough times, eventually you will draw a sample that is representative (i.e., reflective) of the population from which the sample is drawn.

The second determinant of the quality of a data-gathering program is whether or not it allows you to contact a representative sample of your customers. A useful example can be found in the survey research conducted by large polling firms to provide information about political choices, attitudes about controversial topics, and other data relevant to current affairs. These surveys typically range in size from 500 to 1,500 respondents and are usually representative samples of the American public. It is because they are representative samples that the results can be used to say something with 95% confidence about the opinions and behaviors of all adult Americans.

These professional pollsters have some assurance that the sample is representative because it was randomly drawn from the population of interest and is quite large. Probability theory assures us that under these circumstances we will have attained representative ness (within known probabilities) because the characteristics of the sample approximate the characteristics of the population.

Contact center managers should have the same goal for their caller CS measurement programs. The concept of representativeness simply means that along the pre-defined characteristics, the random sample mirrors the characteristics of the population of callers to which you wish to generalize your survey research results. To determine necessary sample sizes refer to figure 71.

Margin of Error

Confidence	10%	5%	3%	2%	1%
80%	41	164	455	1,024	4,096
90%	68	272	756	1,702	6,806
95%	96	384	1,067	2,401	9,604
98%	136	543	1,508	3,393	13,572
99%	166	666	1,849	4,160	16,641

Figure 71. Sampling proportions for large populations

Most companies will have sub-populations within the population of all customers. These segments are more typically called segments and refer to such divergent customer groupings as end-user consumers versus business-to-business customers. Important groups within those sub-populations may also exist. The sampling frame for future phases of the CS program must address these sub-populations by using a stratified random sample.

To illustrate, imagine a computer mail-order house with the customer base segmented into three groups: household, business, and government users. We would want the sample to be drawn from those three segments in proportion to their size since it is likely that each of these three groups has very different customer needs. When this is accomplished, we say that our sample is representative (at least with respect to the limited set of criteria used to segment the customers). It is imperative to collect enough data to satisfy statistical confidence limits. Your measurement program must yield results that are statistically representative of the callers within each group.

This appendix contains important information on how to analyze the external data you have so carefully gathered. The analysis described in this part can be applied to the caller satisfaction survey instrument in Appendix A. Several analytical concepts are presented to enhance the value of the information generated from the data. CS data must be available for analysis in a timely manner. The obvious goal of collecting customer opinions of your service is to make changes to your processes that will increase customer satisfaction. Such changes need to be made quickly in response to market pressures and to avoid further market damage that is caused by a poor service attribute.

Risk Analysis

Another helpful analytic tool is a technique called risk analysis. The theory behind this technique is that the original variables are recoded into just two groups: those with low ratings and those with high ratings. The definition of high and low will vary depending on the number of scale points. Each service attribute variable for which this analysis can be completed does not have to be collapsed to the same scale. Once this grouping is done, the upper left cell are those customers who gave both low ratings to overall satisfaction (or likelihood to continue service) and a specific attribute.

Overall Satisfaction

	1 - 4	5 - 7
Individual 1 - 4	15%	15%
Attributes 5 - 7	10%	60%

Figure 72. Example recoding for vulnerability analysis

With this information in figure 72, you can suggest the following:

1. It was this low attribute rating which contributed to 15% of customers having lower overall satisfaction ratings. Further analysis can identify these customers and a root cause analysis can determine why they rated this service attribute low.

2. The 15% of customers in the upper right cell place little importance on the specific attribute when assigning an overall satisfaction score.

3. The 10% of customers in the lower left cell must rate other attributes poorly to cause the lower overall satisfaction rating.

Vulnerability tables can be generated for any number of measured attributes and a comparison of the percentages in the upper left cell across tables can identify where your risk is greater; i.e., where more customers rate an attribute and overall satisfaction lower.

The technique is called risk analysis because of the assumption that the customers located in the upper left cell are at risk of discontinuing service and that this risk is caused, at least in part, by this specific service attribute. Note that we said in part. Many forces determine customer attitudes, so great reliance should never be placed on a single bivariate analysis except in unusual circumstances such as when performance is so poor (or wonderful) that it dominates all other attributes.

An example of risk analysis is displayed in figure 73. Only 5.6% of the customers appear to be at risk with the vast majority rating both variables at high levels. It is important to realize that the large number of customers in the bottom right cell can also mean that overall quality ratings help cause overall satisfaction. These customers are not at risk and there is no immediate danger of losing them, but we need to keep quality high so that they remain customers. Conversely, there is immediate cause for concern for the 5.6% in the low satisfaction condition.

Overall Satisfaction

Satisfaction with Overall Quality	Lower Overall Satisfaction		Higher Overall Satisfaction	
Lower Satisfaction	28	5.60%	50	18.10%
Higher Satisfaction	56	11.90%	362	17.00%

Figure 73. An example of risk analysis

Scripting, Questions, and Identification of Internal Metrics

Note: Script to be heard by customer appears in quotations.

"Hello, and welcome to _____ 's automated survey. We continue to make service improvements based on the feedback we gather from callers like you. We appreciate your willingness to share your opinion of the service you just received when calling us."

"Please use any number from 1 to 10 to grade the following with 10 being 'most acceptable' and 1 being 'least acceptable.'"

Internal Metric to Be Captured per Call	Customer Perception
# of rings	"The # of rings you heard before the menu choices were presented."
Queue time—ACD answers	"The length of time you spent on hold waiting for the first telephone until advocate answers agent to answer."
Hold time	"During the call, the length of time placed on hold by the telephone agent. If your call was not placed on hold, press 0."
# of transfers	"The need for one agent to transfer you to a different agent to complete your call. If you were not transferred, press 0."

"For the following characteristics, grade the agent using the 1 to 10 scale with 10 being the highest score and 1 being the lowest."

Internal Metric to Be Captured per Call	Customer Perception
# of transfers	"Agent's knowledge of the company's products and services."
Talk time	"Agent spent enough time with you in handling your call."

"Again, with 10 being the highest and 1 being the lowest, rate the following:"

"How satisfied were you with the overall service you received on this call?"

"As a result of this call, how likely are you to continue your service with our company?"

Internal Metric to Be Be Captured per Call	Customer Perception
'First call resolution'	"Did the advocate answer your question or solve your problem during this call? Answer yes or no."

"Thank you very much for your time. Your opinions will be very useful for us in planning the best possible service for you in the future. Good bye."

Additional metrics to be captured from ACD data, or calculated from ACD data concurrent to the call:

- blocked call % at time of call
- abandonment rate at time of call
- time to abandonment at time of call
- after call work time average at time of call
- status of agent (i.e., full-time or part-time and tenure in months)

Simple Regression

The point was made earlier that the customer perception of the operational dimensions of the contact center should be used when setting the service level goals for your contact center. Several types of analyses can provide you with strong, quantitative tools to set these service level goals.

We propose the use of simple linear regression models. Regression is a technique to predict the value of a dependent variable (usually called "y") as follows:

$$y = B0 + B1X + e$$

Where **y** = dependent variable. In the case of a contact center CS survey, this is the caller's perception of the internal metric as seen in the table in Appendix E.

X = independent variable or predictor of y. In the case of a contact center CS survey, these are all the metrics as captured from the ACD at the same time that the caller was on the phone plus any pertinent data from Accounting or Human Resources.

e = random error, it is usually assumed to be 0

B0 = y-intercept of the line through the y-axis

B1 = slope of the line, amount of increase or decrease in y for every 1 unit increase or decrease in **X**.

Repeating from above, the independent variable or X would be the per call actual metrics as captured from the ACD. The dependent variable, or y, is the customer's perception of the metric as rated during the CS survey.

The regression technique plots each X and y pair of values on a coordinate axis. See figure 74 for a plot of data points. In this case, the vertical axis provides the level of the dependent variable (satisfaction with the call) and the horizontal axis the level of the independent variable (actual talk time). The following graphs use a scale from 1 to 5.

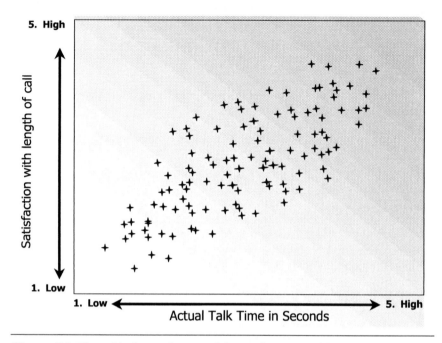

Figure 74. Plot of independent and dependent variable pairs

The intersection of those two levels is the location of that data pair, represented by points on the scatter plot shown in figure 74. For example, on a set of coordinate axes, one axis would indicate the number of minutes of talk time that actually occurred with caller #1 as reported by the ACD (say 3 minutes), and the other axis would indicate caller #1's perception of satisfaction on "spent enough time with you in handling your call" (say very satisfied, or a 5). The intersection of these two levels (3, 5) would be the location of that pair of values. All data pairs are plotted, and then the regression algorithm places a line of best fit through the data. In figure 75, we have added the regression line by using simple statistics. The line is defined by the equation:

$$y = B0 + B1X, \text{ as explained in Appendix E.}$$

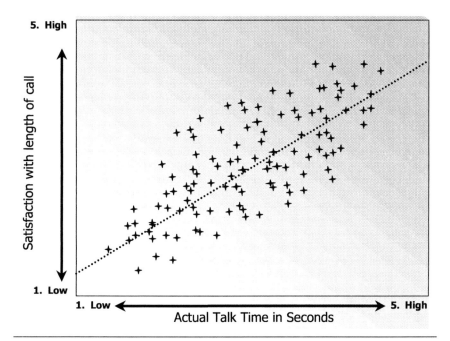

Figure 75. Example of a regression line

Three relationships may exist between the X and y variables. The relationship may be negative (downward sloping with respect to the point of origin) which means that as the independent variable (X) decreases, the dependent variable (y) increases. In this case, B1 (widely known as Beta) is a negative number, so the slope of the line is negative. One would expect a negative relationship in situation where a metric such as "queue time" is too long. An improvement opportunity exists in this case because the satisfaction with "queue time" (y) decreases as actual length of queue time (X) increases.

The relationship may be positive (the line slopes upward with respect to the point of origin) which means that as the independent variable (X) increases the dependent variable (y) increases. In this case, B1 (Beta) is a positive number, which means the slope of the line is upward. One would expect a positive relationship to exist between "satisfaction with spending enough time with the customer" (y) and "talk time" (X). If agents were hurrying to increase their number of calls handled and, therefore, rushing callers off the phone, 'talk time' will decrease, but "satisfaction" will also decrease.

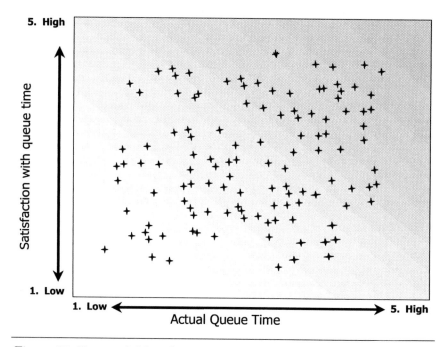

Figure 76. Two variables that are not related

If the two variables were completely unrelated, the true slope of the line (B1) would be zero, which means that X contributes no information for the prediction of y. In this situation, the manager can infer that focusing on that metric will not generate a change in satisfaction. An example of this can be seen in figure 76.

Case Study One

Situation

This case study is based on a situation comparing "time in the queue" as the independent variable (X) and "satisfaction with queue time" as the dependent variable (y). Using the regression results to substitute into the equation, an example for the variable "time in queue" in words would be:

Satisfaction with time in queue = B0 + B1 (actual time in queue)

Using data that has been transformed to a 1 to 5 scale, and inserting the example results we would get: 69 = 92.27 + -1.3 (17.9), where 69 is the average rating of "satisfaction with queue time" (y), and 17.9 seconds (X) is the average actual "time in queue." The B1 (Beta) is negative so the relationship is negative.

Interpretation

If the "time in queue" where reduced by 1 unit (say one second) then the "satisfaction with the time in queue" would increase by 1.3 units (from 69 to 70.3). If the "time in queue" were reduced by 2 seconds, the "satisfaction" would increase by 2.6 units to 71.6. Therefore, reductions in actual "queue time" are predicted to increase perceptions of "satisfaction" in a dependable relationship of 1:1.3.

Case Study Two

Situation

In this example the variables are actual "talk time" versus "satisfaction with the length of the call." For the independent (X) variable "talk time," the equation in words would be:

$$\textit{Satisfaction with talk time} = B0 + B1 \; (\textit{actual talk time})$$

Using data that has been transformed to a 1 to 5 scale, and inserting in the example results: 70 = -6.5 + .17 (450), where 70 is the average rating for "talk time satisfaction" and 450 seconds is the average "talk time" taken from the ACD output.

Interpretation

If the "talk time" was increased by 1 unit (i.e., 1 second) then "satisfaction with talk time" would increase by 0.17 units (from 70 to 70.17). If the "talk time" were increased by 2 seconds, the "satisfaction" would increase by .17 × 2 = .34, so the ratio is 1:0.17.

Note that of the two examples, the second one has a much smaller improvement per unit of change (1:1.3 compared to 1:0.17) between the two independent variables. Looking strictly at these two ratios, it is obvious that talk times should be allowed to increase. But before such a decision can be rationally made, it is important to compute the costs of making changes. It may be that reducing queue time would require system changes that are prohibitively expensive this year, but can be accommodated next year, whereas hiring additional agents and encouraging everyone not to rush callers would be possible this year.

In addition to costs, statistical significance (or impact) needs to be assessed. (See Chapter 4 for discussion and examples). It does no good to make changes that cost only a little money if those changes will not substantially impact your caller satisfaction performance. Better to save the money to use on changes that will substantially impact caller satisfaction.

In conclusion, keep in mind that your focus must be on moving customer satisfaction into the customer delight range, which means achieving a CSI score of 85 or more. As should be clear now, multiple regression and other statistical techniques cannot make managerial decisions: costs, political and other organizational realities, and intuition all play an important part in executive decision-making.

Appendix G: The Importance of Corporate Image

Corporate Image versus Financial Performance

A company's contact center can have a major impact on corporate image. The frequently asked question "Does the public image of a corporation effect the volume of sales of its products or services?" was put to the test in a research conducted at Purdue University's Center for Customer-Driven Quality.

Although the research is still ongoing, initial results reported that in 80% of the Fortune 500 companies studied, the qualitative measure of image is a statistically significant leading indicator of direction of the next year's sales volume. All of the corporate image and sales volume data for the research was taken from *Fortune Magazine* over a period of ten years.

The specific question posed in the Purdue research can best be stated as follows:

"Does an increase or decrease in a company's public image this year have a corresponding increase or decrease in sales volume in the next year or years?"

Quantifying Annual Public Image

Since 1983, Fortune Magazine has published an annual list called "America's Most Admired Companies." Industry experts score their perception of each company on a qualitative scale from zero to ten, where 0 = poor, and 10 = excellent. The companies are judged on eight key attributes of image that impact corporate reputation:

1. Quality of management
2. Quality of products or services
3. Quality of innovation
4. Quality of the company's value as a long-term investment
5. Quality of financial soundness
6. Quality of the work place as seen in the company's ability to attract, develop, and keep talented people

7. Quality of the company's community and environmental actions

8. Quality of the company's planned use of corporate assets

Quantifying the Annual Sales Volume

Fortune Magazine annually publishes the financial data on the "Fortune Top Five Hundred American Companies." This issue contains information for each company including annual sales volume, profits, return on equity, and many other important financial indicators of performance. From this data, the researchers studied the annual sales volume of each selected company.

Results and Conclusions

The results show that over a period of time the change in public image of a company is a statistically significant indicator of the *direction of change* in a company's sales volume, i.e., customers apparently prefer to purchase from companies whose image they admire. The results do not indicate any consistent relationship in the *magnitude* of the changes, just the direction; i.e., if image is up (or down) this year, sales volume is highly likely to be up (or down) next year.

By closely monitoring customer satisfaction and public image, company executives can get an early warning, i.e., a "wake-up call," that next year's sales volumes are going to be impacted by negative word-of-mouth. With this early warning system in place, every possible action should be taken to turn around the situation before the decrease in sales volume occurs with its possible negative effects on profits.

Approximately 20% of the companies studied did not conform to the findings reported, and therefore ongoing research is being conducted to determine what other factors might have influenced these companies to behave differently, i.e., mergers and acquisitions, or new product release that might impact sales volumes.

In conclusion, since corporate image has a high probability of impacting next year's revenue, a world-class contact center can be a major asset for companies.

APPENDIX H: CONTACT CENTER PERFORMANCE BENCHMARKING

Introduction to Performance Comparisons

As discussed in Chapter 3, the contact center is an environment full of data ready to be used for performance measurement and management. In this Appendix we have organized the measurements in groups most useful for measuring different types of performance. In the end, each contact center manager must select from these measurements those that may be most useful and applicable to managing a particular contact center with a specific set of corporate goals.

Contact Center Performance Measurements

- Service Level
- Average Speed of Answer
- Average Time in Queue
- Average Talk Time
- Average Auxiliary Time
- Average After-Call Work Time
- Average Handle Time
- Adherence to Schedule
- Average Abandonment Rate
- Average Time to Abandon
- Retrial Rate
- Agent Utilization
- Average Offered Call Volume Per Hour
- Average Handled Call Volume Per Hour
- Average Blocking Rate
- Revenue-Related Performance Measurements
- Percentage of Time Agents Spend on Calls
- Average Call Value
- Conversion Ratio of Inquiry Calls to Sales
- Average Sales per Agent
- Cost-Related Performance Measurements
- Loaded Cost per Agent
- Average Recruitment Cost
- Average Training Cost

- Average Training Time
- Average Cost per Call
- Average Cost per Order
- Ratio of IVR to Agent-Handled Calls
- Lawsuits Avoided
- Quality of Service Performance Measurements
- Average Tenure of Agents
- Overall Caller Satisfaction
- Number of Complaints or Escalated Calls
- Percent of Calls Requiring Rework
- Complaints Resolved on First Call
- Agent Satisfaction
- Number of Transfers before Resolution

Contact Center Benchmarking

A "benchmark" is a standard of performance or a point of reference from which you can make other measurements. Contact centers lend themselves particularly well to benchmarking because so many elements of a contact center are measured. In fact, it would be fair to say that the company's contact center performance is undoubtedly the most measurable as seen by the many metrics discussed and defined in this book.

In contact centers, benchmarking may take many forms as described below:

1. Against the average of many contact centers in various industries

2. Against the average of many contact centers in the same industry

3. Against the best contact center in various industries

4. Against direct competitors in the same industry

Benchmarking Questionnaire for Customer Service Call Centers

Purdue University
Center for Customer-Driven Quality

In-depth RealityCheck™ Survey

for

Inbound Customer Service Call Centers

Thank you for participating in our research into call center best practices.

In addition to this Survey, we also have in-depth RealityCheck™ Surveys for the following types of centers:

- Outbound Telemarketing
- Outbound Collections
- Inbound Technical Support to External Customers
- Inbound Technical Support to Internal Customers (Help Desk)
- E-mail Handling
- Web-chat Handling
- IVR Call Handling

Please make note of the following regarding this Survey:

1. An inbound call center is defined as any group of telephone Agents whose calls are distributed by an automatic call distributor (ACD) to the next available Agent.

2. Please use one questionnaire for each call center in your company.

3. Your individual performance data will be kept in strict confidence on our secured server.

4. When you have completed this Survey, you may submit your data by one of the following methods:

   - FAX your completed Survey to: (509) 351- 0264, or

   - MAIL your completed Survey to:

     BenchmarkPortal, Inc.
     RealityCheck™ Support
     3201 Airpark Drive, Suite 104
     Santa Maria, CA 93455

GR33-011105

Participant Information

Name _____

Title _____

E-mail Address _____

Company Name _____

Mailing Address _____

City _____ **State** _____ **Zip Code** _____

Phone Number _____ **Extension**_____

FAX Number _____

Toll-Free Number of Your Call Center_____

Referred by:_____ _____

If you have a problem completing your questionnaire, or you have any questions concerning benchmarking, please e-mail the RealityCheck™ Survey Team at:

Inbound.Customer.Service@BenchmarkPortal.com

Or telephone us between 8 AM and 5 PM Pacific Time Monday through Friday at:

(805) 614-0123 extension 12

Or call **Dr. Jon Anton** at Purdue University:

(765) 494-8357

From the Industry Groups Below, Please Circle One
Industry that Best Represents Your Company

Banking/Finance:
  Banking
  Brokerage
  Credit Card
  Mortgage
  Other
Consumer Products:
  Electronics
  Food/Beverage
  Health/Beauty
  Pet supplies
  Other
Government:
  Federal
  Municipal
  State
Healthcare/Pharmaceutical:
  Healthcare Provider
  Pharmaceuticals
  Other
Information Technology:
  Computer Hardware
  Computer Software
  Other
Insurance:
  Health
  Life
  Property/Casualty
  Other
Manufacturing/Chemicals/
Construction:
  Aerospace
  Automotive
  Building Materials/
    Construction
  Chemicals
  Other

Media:
  Radio
  Publishing
  Television
  Other
Retail/Catalog:
  Catalog
  Online
  Retail Store
  Other
Transportation:
  Public Transportation
    Systems
  Rail
  Toll Road
  Trucking
Telecommunications:
  Cable/Broadband/Satellite
  Voice
  Data/Internet Service
    Provider
  Wireless
  Other
Travel:
  Airline
  Hotel/Resort/Cruise Line
  Travel Agency
  Other
Utilities/Fuel:
  Gas
  Electric
  Electric and Gas
  Fuel Oil
  Other
Other (Please specify:
_____)

Call Center Profile for Peer Group Classification

1. **How many inbound calls per year are directed to your call center?**

   Calls offered annually ⎯⎯⎯⎯

   (Calls offered is the total number of calls you receive in a given year. This number is provided by your ACD.)

2. **Of the inbound calls directed to your call center, how many are handled by a live Agent and/or your IVR?**

   Calls handled annually ⎯⎯⎯⎯

   (Calls handled are the number of calls you actually completed by a live Agent, plus calls handled by your IVR. Calls handled must be equal to, or less than calls offered.) This number is provided by your ACD.

3. **Of all the calls handled annually by your center, how do they breakdown into the following two categories?**

   Annual call volume handled by your Agents ⎯⎯⎯⎯

   Annual call volume handled completely by your IVR ⎯⎯⎯⎯

   ("Completely by your IVR" means that the call did not require a live Agent to complete the call and therefore, it was handled by caller "self service.")

4. **Of the calls handled annually by your Agents, how do they breakdown in the following two categories?**

   Business to business ⎯⎯⎯⎯%
   (Fill in the percentage of calls handled that came from a business customer.)

   Business to consumer ⎯⎯⎯⎯%
   (Fill in the percentage of calls handled that came from an individual consumer, also known as an "end user.")

   Total 100 %

5. **How many minutes of telephone usage are recorded annually by your call center's automatic call distributor (ACD)?**

   ⎯⎯⎯⎯

6. How many Agents work at your call center?

Full-time Agents   _____
(Fill in the number of full-time Agents employed in your call center.)

Part-time Agents   _____
(Fill in the number of part-time Agents employed in your call center.)

7. How many Full Time Equivalent Agents (FTE) work at your call center?

Full-time Equivalents (FTEs)   _____
(FTE= Total Agent payroll hours per week divided by 40. A full-time Agent equals 1.0 FTE's. A part-time Agent who works 20 hours a week (half that of a full-time Agent) equals 0.5 FTE.)

8. Are your Agents represented by a labor union?

☐   Yes
☐   No

9. If your Agents do more than just answer inbound calls, what other functions do they perform?

Agent Functions	Average Percent of Agent Time
Inbound Calls	_____
Outbound Call	_____
Respond to E-mails	_____
Answer On-line Web-chats	_____
Other	_____

If other, please specify:

_____

10. Which of the following types of calls do your Agents handle as a percent of their total calls handled?

a. Customer Service   _____%
   (Providing callers with quick and accurate answers to their questions, and/or logging and updating customer information.)

b. Order Taking and Order Tracking   _____%
   (Taking and tracking orders for products and/or services.)

c. Technical Support to External Customers _____%
   (Handling product-use questions and "fix-it" questions for external customers (if the percentage of support calls is over 50%, you should complete our Technical Support Survey, not this one.))

d. Complaints   _____%
   (Handling customer complaints.)

e. Re-directing Inbound Calls   _____%
   (Routing callers to next available specialist.)

f. Other   _____%
   (Fill in the percentage of calls handled that are a type other than any of the options provided above.)

If other, please describe:

_____

Total   **100 %**

Call Center Costs

11. What is the total annual budget for your call center for this year?

(Fill in the annual operating budget allocated for your call center for this year.)

$_____

12. How do you compensate your Agents?

(Average hourly wage for front-line Agents.)

$_____

13. What is your average cost per call in dollars?

(This is the sum of all costs for running the call center for the period, divided by the number of calls handled in the call center for the same period. This would include all calls whether handled by an Agent or by the IVR.)

$_____

Call Center Performance Measures

14. Over the past 90 days, what were your average inbound performance time-based metrics?

a. 80% of your calls are answered in how many seconds _____

(This is (the number of calls answered in X seconds) divided by (offered calls) times 100.)

b. Average speed of answer in seconds _____

(This is the total queue time, divided by the number of calls handled. This includes both IVR-handled calls as well as calls handled by a live Agent.)

c. Average talk time in minutes (includes hold time) _____

(This is the average amount of time an Agent spends talking with a customer during the course of one phone call.)

d. Average after call work time in minutes _____

(This is the average amount of time an Agent spends on performing follow-up work after the Agent has disconnected from the caller.)

e. Average time in queue in seconds _____

(This is the average wait time that a caller endures. This differs from average speed of answer because this calculation includes only calls that actually had a wait time. This metric is also known as average time of delay.)

f. Average time before abandoning in seconds _____

(This is the average amount of time a customer will wait in queue before abandoning.)

15. Over the past 90 days, what were your average inbound performance percentage-based metrics?

a. Average abandoned in percent _____

(This is the percentage of calls that get connected to the ACD, but get disconnected by the caller before reaching an Agent, or before completing a process within the IVR.)

b. Calls resolved on first call in percent _____

(This is the percentage of calls that were completely resolved during the course of the first inbound call initiated by the customer, and therefore do not require a call back.)

c. Calls blocked in percent   _____
(These are calls that never make it to your ACD. Examples of blocked calls are: "busy signals," "number not in service" messages, etc. This number can be provided only by your telecommunications provider.)

d. Agent occupancy in percent   _____
(This is the percentage of time that an Agent is in their seat connected to the ACD, and either engaged in a call or ready to answer a call as compared to the total number of hours at work.)

e. Adherence to schedule in percent   _____
(This percentage represents how closely an Agent adheres to his/her detailed work schedule as provided by the workforce management system. 100% adherence means that the Agent was exactly where they were supposed to be at the time projected in their schedule. The scheduled time allows for meetings with the supervisor, education, plus answering customer phone calls.)

f. Average attendance in percent   _____
(This is a percentage representing how often an Agent is NOT absent from work due to an unplanned absence (not to include excused absences, i.e., vacation, FMLA, jury duty, etc.). Take the total number of unexcused absences and divide it by the total number of days that the Agent was expected to be at work, and subtract that number from 100.)

g. Average calls transferred in percent   _____
(This represents the percent of calls transferred from the original Agent that connects with the customer.)

h. Average caller hold time in seconds while on the phone with an Agent   _____
(This is the average amount of time, in seconds, that callers are on hold after being connected to an Agent. Most ACD systems provide this number.)

i. Average Auxiliary (Aux) Time in percent   _____
(This is the average amount of time per shift, in percent, that an Agent is logged into an Aux state. This should include all authorized off-line time, i.e. time set aside for handling emails, training, or other job-related tasks.)

j. Average Utilization in percent   _____
(Agent utilization is the percentage of time that an Agent is in their seat ready to handle calls as compared to the actual time they are in telephone mode. Utilization equals the product of average call

handle time (talk time + hold time + after call work time) and the average number of inbound calls per Agent per 8-hour shift (ACPS), divided by total time the Agent is connected to the ACD and ready to handle calls during a shift, i.e., occupancy (not in percent).)

$$Utilization = \frac{(ATT + ACW)(ACPS)}{Occupancy} X100$$

16. **How many inbound calls per hour are handled by your Agents?**
(This is the average number of calls that an Agent handles per hour.)

_____

17. **Does your call center have a formal process to collect the caller's satisfaction regarding their experience with how their call was handled?**

☐ Yes
☐ No

18. **On average, in the past 90 days what percentage of your callers gave you a perfect score on the question, "Overall, how satisfied were you with the service you received during your call to our center?"**
(a "highest" score of 5 out of 5, or the top of whatever scale you use)

_____%

19. **On average, in the past 90 days, what percentage of your callers gave you the lowest score on the question, "Overall, how satisfied were you with the service you received during your call to our company?"**
(a "lowest" score of 1 out of 5, or the top of whatever scale you use)

_____%

20. **Does your call center have a formal mechanism for gathering Agent feedback?**
(Does your call center gather both positive and/or negative feedback from your Agents?)

☐ Yes
☐ No

21. **On average, in the past 90 days, what percentage of your Agents gave you a perfect score on the question, "Overall, how satisfied are you with your position?"**
    (a "highest" score of 5 out of 5, or the top of whatever scale you use)

    _____%

22. **On average, in the past 90 days, what percentage of your Agents gave you the lowest score on the question, "Overall, how satisfied are you with your position?"**
    (a "lowest" score of 1 out of 5, or the bottom of whatever scale you use)

    _____%

23. **What is the ratio of agents to supervisors (span of control)?**

    Agents per supervisor   _____
    (Fill in how many Agents, on average, you have assigned to each supervisor.)

24. **What is the annual percentage turnover of your full-time Agents?**

    _____

25. **As a percentage of total turnover (Question 24 above), how does this breakdown into the following two categories?**

    Promotional turnover   _____
    (This is the turnover caused by promotions within the call center from Agent to some other position in the call center, and/or promotions where Agents go to other departments within the company.)

    All Other Turnover   _____
    (This is all other turnover not related to promotions, but related to and including voluntary and involuntary termination.)

26. **Of your calls handled by the IVR, what percent of callers opt out to a live Agent?**

    _____%

Benchmarking Questionnaire for Inbound E-mail Contact Centers

Purdue University
Center for Customer-Driven Quality

E-mail Benchmark Questionnaire

Thank you for participating in our research into contact center performance levels. Please make note of the following:

1. Please use one questionnaire for each customer contact facility.

2. A contact center handles e-mails, and/or telephone calls (inbound or outbound), and/or Web site requests.

3. Your individual performance data will be kept in strict confidence on our secured server.

4. You will receive a free executive summary report comparing your performance against others in the database. This report will be sent to you by e-mail within approximately two to three weeks from the time you complete entering all of your data.

5. When you have completed your questionnaire, you may submit your data by one of the following methods:

    *   Visit our Web site at www.BenchmarkPortal.com, create a new account or login to your existing account, and enter the questionnaire data online

    *   FAX your completed survey to (805) 614-0055 for entry into the database

    *   MAIL your completed survey to:

        BenchmarkPortal, Inc.
        3201 Airpark Drive, Suite 104
        Santa Maria, CA 93455

This questionnaire was created on 02/19/02

Participant Account Information
(Required for FAX or mail questionnaire submissions)

Name _____

E-mail Address _____

Company Name _____

Mailing Address _____

City _____ **State** _____ **Zip Code** _____

Phone Number _____ **Ext.** _____

FAX Number _____

Company Web site _____

Contact Center E-mail Address _____

Are you having a problem completing your questionnaire, or do you have questions concerning benchmarking? Please e-mail the Benchmark Survey Team at:

Information@BenchmarkPortal.com

Or telephone us between 8 AM and 4 PM Pacific Time Monday through Friday at:

(805) 614-0123 ext. 16

You may also obtain further help with benchmarking by calling **Dr. Jon Anton** at Purdue University:

(765) 494-8357

Classification

1. **What is your total e-mail volume per month (exclusive of internal e-mail)?**

   Inbound e-mail volume per month _____

   Outbound e-mail volume per month _____

2. **What percentage of your total e-mail volume is secured?**
   - ☐ Between 0 - 25%
   - ☐ Between 26 - 50%
   - ☐ Between 51 - 75%
   - ☐ Between 76 - 100%
   - ☐ Don't use secured

3. **Which of the following functions do your Agents provide regarding e-mail contacts?**

Buying / bidding	_____%
Selling / listing	_____%
Registration	_____%
Customer service (questions and inquiries)	_____%
Technical support – external	_____%
Site issues	_____%
Order taking and tracking	_____%
Information requests	_____%
Public relations	_____%
Complaint resolution	_____%
Other	_____%
Total	**100 %**

4. **How do your inbound e-mails break down in the following categories:**

Business to business	_____%
Business to consumer	_____%
Consumer to consumer	_____%
Total	**100 %**

5. **Do you use an automatic e-mail response system at your contact center?**
   - ☐ Yes
   - ☐ No

6. How many Agents work at your contact center?

Full-time Agents _____

Part-time Agents _____

Contract Agents _____

Full-time Equivalents (FTEs)

(FTE = Total payroll hours per week divided by 40 hours per week)

Customer Contact Center Costs

7. What is the total annual budget for your contact center?
(Include everything that is mentioned in the next question.)

Last year $_____

This year $_____

Next year $_____

8. What percentage of your ongoing cost is for:

Human Resources - salary, benefits, etc.   _____%

Human Resources - recruiting, screening, training   _____%

Telecommunications Line Charge   _____%

Computer Hardware   _____%

Computer Software   _____%

Telecommunications Equipment   _____%

Real Estate (floor space)   _____%

Outsourced contracts   _____%

Other   _____%

Total   100 %

9. What is your fully loaded cost per e-mail in dollars?

Cost per e-mail in dollars $_____

10. What percentage of your annual revenue is your fully loaded annual e-mail cost?

_____%

Performance Measurement

11. What percentage of e-mail contacts are answered in how many hours?

Less than 2 hours	_____%
Between 2 - 4 hours	_____%
Between 4 - 6 hours	_____%
Between 6 - 8 hours	_____%
Between 8 - 12 hours	_____%
Between 12 - 24 hours	_____%
Between 24 - 36 hours	_____%
Greater than 36 hours	_____%
Total	**100 %**

12. What is your service level goal for e-mail response? (percentage handled in how many hours)

Within 2 hours	_____%
Within 4 hours	_____%
Within 6 hours	_____%
Within 8 hours	_____%
Within 12 hours	_____%
Within 24 hours	_____%
Within 36 hours	_____%

13. What are your inbound e-mail service level statistics?

Average Agent time per e-mail in minutes	_____minutes
Contacts resolved on first e-mail response in percent	_____%
Average number of e-mail contacts per resolution	_____
Agent occupancy in percent	_____%
Adherence to schedule in percent	_____%
Average attendance in percent	_____%
Cost per contact transaction in dollars	$_____
Average sale value in dollars	$_____
Average e-mail contacts handled per hour per Agent	_____
Average e-mail contacts handled per 8-hour shift per Agent	_____

Performance Measurement

14. What percentage of your e-mail volume is repeat e-mail to the same customer trying to solve the same problem or answer the same question?

Percentage of re-sent e-mails _____%

15. What is your e-mail error rate (number of errors per 1000 e-mails)?

(An error is a mistake or action that requires human intervention to correct.)

Errors per 1000 e-mails _____

16. Does your contact center do any up-selling/cross-selling?

☐ Yes
☐ No

17. What percentage of contacts give rise to up-selling/cross-selling opportunities?

_____%

18. What is your average sale value per up-sell/cross-sell in dollars?

$_____

19. What is the primary indicator of your e-mail associates' productivity?

☐ E-mail responses per hour
☐ E-mail responses per shift
☐ Average processing time per response
☐ Do not measure associates' e-mail productivity
☐ Other

20. Please specify the "other" indicator of your e-mail associates' productivity:

_____

Satisfaction Measurement

21. **Does your contact center have a formal mechanism for gathering customer feedback on contact center performance?**

    ☐ Yes
    ☐ No

22. **What percentage of your customer contacts gives you a percent score?**

    (e.g., a perfect score of 5 out of 5, or a perfect score of 7 out of 7)

    _____%

23. **What percentage of contacts to the center result in a complaint about how a previous e-mail was handled?**

    _____%

Human Resource Management

24. What percentage of Agents work at each level in your contact center?

Level one _____%

Level two _____%

Level three _____%

Level four and higher _____%

25. If more than four levels of Agents work in your contact center, please specify the number of levels?

_____

26. What is the ratio of Agents to supervisors (span of control)?

Agents per supervisor _____

27. What is the annual turnover of your inbound Agent staff?

(including both internal transfers and external attrition)

Full-time _____%

Part-time _____%

28. How do you compensate your Agents?

Base salary per year only $_____

Per hour only $_____

29. What is the average annual salary of your supervisors?

$_____

30. What is the average annual salary of your contact center manager?

$_____

31. What is the length (in hours) of your initial, new-hire training period for Agents?

_____hours

32. How much does it cost you to bring on a new Agent (including recruiting, screening, training)?

New Agent hiring cost in dollars $_____

33. Do you have a specific hiring/selection process for an associate's e-mail related skills?

☐ Yes
☐ No
☐ Don't know

Human Resource Management

34. Are your Agents represented by a labor union?

☐ Yes
☐ No

35. What percentage of your total contact volume is handled by part-time Agents?

_____%

Process & Knowledge

36. Of your customer service e-mail messages, what percentage are:

Automatically routed to the appropriate Agent from Web site	_____%
Automatically routed to the appropriate Agent from e-mail system (non-Web form e-mail)	_____%
Manually routed to the appropriate Agent	_____%

37. Is the software application you use to process e-mail messages:

☐ Proprietary
☐ Commercial

38. If a commercial software application is used to process e-mail messages, what vendor do you use?

_____

39. Of your automated responses, what percentage of your e-mail messages are serviced using:

Templates	_____%
Form letters	_____%
Form paragraphs	_____%
Free-form responses	_____%
Auto-acknowledge	_____%
Auto-suggest	_____%
Auto-response	_____%
Other	_____%
Total	**100 %**

40. What is your average e-mail turnover time per response?

Turnaround in hours _____hours

41. What percentage of e-mail responses are undeliverable?

_____%

42. **What are your hours of operation for handling e-mail messages?**

Number of hours per weekday, Monday through Friday   _____

Number of hours per Saturday   _____

Number of hours per Sunday   _____

Number of hours per Holiday   _____

43. **On average, what percentage of your e-mail associates' time is spent performing some other function?**

☐ Between 0 - 25%

☐ Between 26 - 50%

☐ Between 51 - 75%

☐ Between 76 - 100%

☐ E-mail associates do not perform other functions

44. **Is the contact center integrated with other customer access touchpoints?**

(for instance, phone, Web site, FAX-back, kiosk)

☐ Yes
☐ No

45. **On the Internet, which alternate touchpoints does your Web site offer?** *(check all that apply)*

☐ Your contact center's 1-800 number

☐ A self-service option (e.g., a static FAQ section)

☐ Voice Over IP, or Internet contact

☐ Instant Messaging (chat capabilities)

☐ Discussion boards, voice groups, etc.

46. **Of all your inbound contacts, what percentage is handled by self-service?**

_____%

Quality Management

47. How do you measure quality? *(check all that apply)*

- ☐ By sampling
- ☐ Number of e-mails required to solve one customer request
- ☐ Error rate per associate
- ☐ Error rate per 1000 responses for center
- ☐ We do not measure quality
- ☐ We use an external company to measure quality
- ☐ Other

48. Please specify the name of the external company used to measure quality:

49. How often do you measure the quality of each associate's e-mail responses (excluding escalations)?

- ☐ Daily
- ☐ Weekly
- ☐ Bi-weekly
- ☐ Monthly
- ☐ Quarterly
- ☐ Other

50. How often do you review the quality of each Agent's e-mail responses with the Agent (excluding escalations)?

- ☐ Daily
- ☐ Weekly
- ☐ Bi-weekly
- ☐ Monthly
- ☐ Quarterly
- ☐ Other

Outsourcing

51. Does your center outsource any contacts or functions?

☐ Yes
☐ No

52. What percentage of your total contacts do you outsource?

_____%

Facilities and Design

53. What is the total number of Agent workstations at your contact center?

Seats   _____

54. What percentage of your workstations are used by more than one Agent per day (desk sharing)?

_____%

55. How large is your average Agent cubical workspace?

Square feet   _____

56. How many total square feet does your contact center occupy?

Square feet   _____

Additional Metrics

57. Are there additional metrics and/or key performance indicators that you would like to have included in this questionnaire?
☐ Yes
☐ No

58. Please enter additional metric or key performance indicator you would like to have included in this questionnaire:

_____

59. Please enter additional metric or key performance indicator you would like to have included in this questionnaire:

_____

60. Please enter additional metric or key performance indicator you would like to have included in this questionnaire:

_____

Benchmarking Information

This appendix includes interesting contact center benchmarking information from a study conducted by Purdue University and sponsored by Axiom, a division of Cambridge Technology Partners. The summary data represents benchmarking results from approximately 300 contact centers across industries. The tables have been arranged by industry as follows:

1. Computer   =   High-tech (hardware and software) companies
2. Telecommunications   =   Network & cellular providers
3. Utilities   =   Electrical, gas, and water utilities
4. Banking   =   Financial services companies
5. Insurance   =   Insurance providers
6. Manufacturing   =   Physical product manufacturers
7. Health   =   Health maintenance organizations and hospitals
8. Transport   =   Airline, trucking, & railway companies

Contact center benchmark data lets you expand beyond just looking at your own performance measurements. The data in this appendix gives you a way to compare your center's performance with levels achieved by other contact centers in your industry. The data presented should be a handy way to determine whether your contact center is performing better than, worse than, or similar to other contact centers.

Remember that the data presented are only averages. You may choose not to meet these average performance measurements because your goals may be higher, depending on your specific contact center goals.

Performance by Industry:

	Cost per Call	Cost per Minute	Cost per Agent	% Perfect Score
All Industries (Overall)	$6.59	$3.04	$68,348	54.39%
Banks	$4.25	$4.17	$70,363	52.94%
Computer Hardware and Software	$10.93	$3.51	$135,722	53.71%
Health Care	$6.25	$1.99	$56,784	63.43%
Insurance	$6.67	$2.11	$68,443	53.25%
Telecommunications	$7.36	$4.61	$75,955	36.50%
Transportation	$7.69	$1.55	$78,877	49.10%
Utilities	$6.04	$1.63	$76,442	63.57%
Miscellaneous	$6.41	$3.05	$67,648	54.81%

Performance by Contact Center Type:

	Cost per Call	Cost per Minute	Cost per Agent	% Perfect Score
Route calls	$4.76	$1.54	$66,363	71.30%
Complaint resolution	$6.31	$1.99	$70,552	12.67%
Consumer affairs	$5.41	$4.08	$59,621	68.80%
Customer service	$5.41	$2.63	$65,193	60.98%
Dispatching	$5.60	$4.78	$70,025	64.90%
Technical Support Internal	$11.75	$2.69	$65,400	59.52%
Inside Sales	$7.11	$4.51	$98,256	45.00%
Order Taking & Tracking	$6.23	$1.76	$63,302	64.11%
Information Requests	$2.25	$7.31	$39,229	53.97%
Technical Support External	$12.98	$4.54	$93,568	45.77%
Other	$3.11	$1.18	$78,482	38.50%

Contact Center Statistics by Industry:

	ASA (in seconds)	AHT (in minutes)	ABAND (in percent)	QUEUE (in seconds)
All Industries (Overall)	34.09	10.10	5.35	36.45
Banks	38.07	7.65	5.27	34.94
Computer Hardware and Software	75.59	18.45	7.31	50.06
Health Care	25.64	8.30	6.71	40.75
Insurance	27.66	10.26	4.58	30.52
Telecommunications	19.70	7.36	5.72	62.25
Transportation	26.50	91.50	5.25	30.50
Utilities	54.20	4.70	6.43	65.64
Miscellaneous	29.36	9.00	5.08	31.53

	Closed on First Contact (in percent)	Agent Available Time (in hours)	After-Call Work Time (in minutes)	Turnover in Agent Staff (full-time) (in percent)
All Industries (Overall)	67.96	74.25	4.86	25.21
Banks	66.69	76.23	4.01	17.68
Computer Hardware and Software	50.57	76.18	7.98	22.16
Health Care	81.78	68.04	3.82	17.92
Insurance	70.99	75.60	4.06	25.70
Telecommunications	70.55	77.72	3.03	18.46
Transportation	81.50	83.00	2.00	27.00
Utilities	46.33	65.00	1.78	20.37
Miscellaneous	70.15	73.35	5.30	29.18

Anton, J., & Gustin, D (2000). *Call Center Benchmarking: How Good is Good Enough*. West Lafayette: Ichor Business Books.

Anton, J. (1997). *Call Center Management: By the Numbers*. West Lafayette: Ichor Business Books.

Anton, J. (1997). *The Voice of the Customer*. The Customer Service Group, New York, NY.

Anton, J., et al. (1996). *Customer Relationship Management*. Prentice-Hall, New York, NY.

Anton, J., & Johns, B. (1996). *Contact Center Best Practice Benchmarking*. Purdue University Center for Customer-Driven Quality, West Lafayette, IN.

Anton, J. (1996). "Is Your Contact Center an Asset or Liability?" *Support Solutions Magazine*, January.

Anton, J. (1996). "Quality of Service Standards." *Support Solutions Magazine*, May.

Anton, J. (1996). "Quality of Service Measurements." *Support Solutions Magazine*, June.

Anton, J. (1995). *Contact Center Best Practice Benchmarking*. Purdue University Center for Customer-Driven Quality, West Lafayette, IN.

Anton, J. (1994). *Corporate Mission Statements and Customer Satisfaction*. Purdue University Center for Customer-Driven Quality, West Lafayette, IN.

Anton, J., et al. (1994). *Call Center Design and Implementation*. Dame Publications, Houston, TX.

Anton, J., & de Ruyter, J.C. (1991). "Van Klachten naar Managementinformatie." *Harvard Holland Business Review*, p27.

Bell, R. (1994). *Customers as Partners: Building Relationships that Last*. Kohler Publishers, Inc.

Bitner, M.J., et al. (1990). "The Service Encounter." *The Journal of Marketing*.

Bolesh, Eric (2001) *Call Center Excellence: Continuous Improvement Boosts Performance*; PR Newswire, ProQuest Direct, New York, NY.

Burgers, A., & Anton J. (1990). *The Impact of Image on Revenue*. Purdue University Center for Customer-Driven Quality, West Lafayette, IN.

Reichfield, F.F. (1993). "Loyalty-Based Management." *The Harvard Business Review*.

Rust, R., et al. (1994). *Return on Quality*. Probus Publishing, Chicago, IL.

Co-Author

Dr. Jon Anton (also known as "Dr. Jon") is the director of benchmark research at Purdue University's Center for Customer-Driven Quality. He specializes in enhancing customer service strategy through inbound call centers, and e-business centers, using the latest in telecommunications (voice), and computer (digital) technology. He also focuses on using the Internet for external customer access, as well as Intranets and middleware.

Since 1995, Dr. Jon has been the principal investigator of the Purdue University Call Center Benchmark Research. This data is now collected at the BenchmarkPortal.com Web site, where it is placed into a data warehouse that currently contains over ten million data points on call center performance. Based on the analysis of this data, Dr. Jon authors the following monthly publications: "The Purdue Page" in *Call Center Magazine*, "Dr. Jon's Benchmarks" in *Call Center News*, "Dr. Jon's Industry Statistics" in *Customer Interface Magazine*, and "Dr. Jon's Business Intelligence" in the *Call Center Manager's Report*.

Dr. Jon has assisted over 400 companies in improving their customer service strategy/delivery by the design and implementation of inbound and outbound call centers, as well as in the decision-making process of using teleservice providers for maximizing service levels while minimizing costs per call. In August of 1996, *Call Center Magazine* honored Dr. Jon by selecting him as an Original Pioneer of the emerging call center industry. In October of 2000, Dr. Jon was named to the Call Center Hall of Fame. In January of 2001, Dr. Jon was selected for the industry's "Leaders and Legends" Award by Help Desk 2000. Dr. Jon is also a member of the National Committee for Quality Assurance.

Dr. Jon has guided corporate executives in strategically re-positioning their call centers as robust customer access centers through a combination of benchmarking, re-engineering, consolidation, outsourcing, and Web-enablement. The resulting single point of contact for the customer allows business to be conducted anywhere, anytime, and in any form. By better understanding the customer lifetime value, Dr. Jon has developed techniques for calculating the ROI for customer service initiatives.

Dr. Jon has published 96 papers on customer service and call center methods in industry journals. In 1997, one of his papers on self-service was awarded the best article of the year by *Customer Relationship Management Magazine*.

Dr. Jon has published twenty-three professional books:

1. *Contact Center Management "By The Numbers"*, The Anton Press, 2005

2. *Managing Web-Based Customer Experiences: Self-service Integrated with Assisted Service*, The Anton Press, 2003

3. *From Cost to Profit Center: How Technology Enables the Difference*, The Anton Press, 2003

4. *Customer Service and the Human Experience: We, the People, Make a Difference*, The Anton Press, 2003

5. *Customer Service at a Crossroads: What You Do Next to Improve Performance Will Determine Your Company's Destiny*, The Anton Press, 2003

6. *Offshore Outsourcing Opportunities*, The Anton Press, 2002

7. *Optimizing Outbound Calling: The Strategic Use of Predictive Dialers*, The Anton Press, 2002

8. *Customer Relationship Management Technology: Building the Infrastructure for Customer Collaboration*, The Anton Press, 2002

9. *Customer Obsession: Your Roadmap to Profitable CRM*, The Anton Press, 2002

10. *Integrating People with Process and Technology: Gaining Employee Acceptance of Technology Initiatives*, The Anton Press, 2002

11. *Selecting a Teleservices Partner: Sales, Service, and Support*, The Anton Press, 2002

12. *How to Conduct a Call Center Performance Audit: A to Z,* The Anton Press, 2002

13. *20:20 CRM A Visionary Insight into Unique Customer Contact,* The Anton Press, 2001

14. *Minimizing Agent Turnover: The Biggest Challenge for Customer Contact Centers,* The Anton Press, 2001

15. *e-Business Customer Service: The Need for Quality Assessment,* The Anton Press, 2001

16. *Customer Relationship Management, The Bottom Line to Optimizing Your ROI,* Prentice Hall, 2nd Edition, 2001

17. *Call Center Performance Enhancement Using Simulation and Modeling,* Purdue University Press, 2000

18. *Call Center Benchmarking: How Good is "Good Enough",* Purdue University Press, 1999

19. *Listening to the Voice of the Customer,* Alexander Communications, 1997

20. *Contact Center Management by the Numbers,* Purdue University Press, 1997

21. *Customer Relationship Management: Making Hard Decisions with Soft Numbers,* Prentice-Hall, Inc., 1996

22. *Inbound Customer Contact Center Design,* Dame Publishers, Inc., 1994

23. *Computer-Assisted Learning,* Hafner Publishing, Inc., 1985

Dr. Jon is the editor for a series of professional books entitled *Customer Access Management,* published by the Purdue University Press.

Dr. Jon's formal education was in technology, including a Doctorate of Science and a Master of Science from Harvard University, a Master of Science from the University of Connecticut, and a Bachelor of Science from the University of Notre Dame. He also completed a three-summer intensive Executive Education program in Business at the Graduate School of Business at Stanford University.

Dr. Jon can be reached at 765.494.8357 or at <DrJonAnton@BenchmarkPortal.com>.

Co-Author

Kamál Webb is Director of Benchmarking Practices and Manager of Help Desk Operations at BenchmarkPortal. In this capacity, he works with companies to benchmark and improve their contact center performance up to a level where they can attain the coveted Purdue University Center for Customer-Driven Quality Certification as a "Center of Excellence." Kamál is a Purdue Certified Contact Center Auditor, and BenchmarkPortal Certified Benchmarking Instructor and Analyst.

Kamál has been the engagement leader and consultant on over 200 benchmarking studies and has assisted in the research of numerous customized benchmarking reports, research studies, and white papers.

Kamál's background includes experience as a front-line agent, team leader, call center trainer, supervisor, and manager. He has brought this experience to bear on his work, performing call center best practice assessments and certification. Kamál's professional education includes undergraduate work at the University of Phoenix.

Content Editor

John Chatterley is Senior Content Editor and Director of Research at BenchmarkPortal, Inc. John has published numerous customized benchmarking reports, research reports, One-Minute Survey reports, and White Papers. Mr. Chatterley co-authored books entitled "Offshore Outsourcing Opportunities," "Selecting a Teleservices Partner," and "Automated Self-Service Using Speech Recognition," and is currently working on several others. Mr. Chatterley is also writer/editor of the annual series of 42 detailed industry reports covering the spectrum of contact center industry sectors. He authored a comprehensive White Paper study entitled "Improving Contact Center Performance through Optimized Site Selection."

John's professional career spans more than 20 years of experience in call center management and consulting. John is a Purdue Certified Contact Center Auditor, Certified AT&T Call Center College Instructor, BenchmarkPortal Certified Benchmarking Instructor and Analyst.

A

abandon rate, 3, 59, 62, 77,
106, 180, 181, 199, 204, 205
access points, 4, 13, 14, 95
ACD, 33, 35, 37, 40, 43, 44, 46,
48, 50–64, 66, 67, 68, 69, 72,
77, 100, 101, 112, 136, 143,
151, 162, 182, 199–206,
221–24, 227
actionable reports, 105
adherence, 43
adherence monitoring devices,
41
after call work time, 44
agent
compensation, 124
development, 124
expectations, 177
hiring process, 123
performance measurement,
158
satisfaction, 187
skill development, 159
staffing, 17, 144, 151
turnover, 15, 69, 123, 196
AHT, 48, 145, 146, 263
Anton, Jon, ix, 111, 194
Anton's Hierarchy of Caller
Needs, 88
ASA, 55, 106, 142, 178, 180,
200, 263
assessment
and certification, 121
discovery, 127
findings and
recommendations, 126
next steps recommendations,
128

automatic call distributors. *See*
ACD
average
abandonment time, 46
after call work time, 180
cost per call/contact, 46
entry error rate, 72
handle time, 48. *See* AHT
hold time, 49
number of rings, 51
queue time, 52
talk time, 3, 55, 56, 112, 180

B

balanced score card report, 126
benchmark performance matrix,
125
benchmarking, x, 11, 19, 34, 42,
99, 100, 109, 110–20, 113,
115, 116, 117, 129, 130, 192,
231, 232, 233, 244, 261, 265,
269, 270, 271
BenchmarkPortal, x, 18, 87, 91,
110, 114, 120, 121, 122, 129,
187, 192
best practices, 141, 149, 154,
159, 162, 163, 166, 168, 170,
172, 173, 175, 177, 180
big picture, 105
bottom box C-sat, 73

C

call center assessment, 119
call handling characteristics,
165
call management systems, 145
call monitoring, 45, 90, 159,
165, 169
call monitoring and agent
coaching process, 124

273

BENCHMARKPORTAL'S PRODUCTS AND SERVICES LISTING

To further our mission of providing contact center leaders with the tools they need to improve the efficiency and effectiveness of their contact centers, we offer the following products and services.

1. RealityCheck™

RealityCheck™ is a free Web-based tool that allows contact centers to assess the effectiveness and efficiency of their current contact center performance as compared to those in the same industry.

RealityCheck™ includes a Balanced Performance Matrix, which plots your efficiency and effectiveness against your industry peers. Call quantity (efficiency) is plotted on the x-axis. Call quality (effectiveness) is plotted on the y-axis; combined, these provide you with a high-level view of your call center performance.

Call centers that are able to optimize customer-centric results, while containing costs are "Call Centers of Excellence;" these are centers positioned in the most desirable upper-right quadrant.

Recommended for: All contact centers. Centers that do not have sufficient analytical staff are encouraged, but not required, to use a Purdue-certified consultant (see Web site) to help them with data gathering and report interpretation. Centers with their own analytical staff should consider sending their specialist to us for training in the proper use of our benchmarking reports.

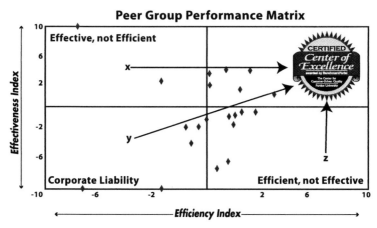

To access RealityCheck™, go to www.BenchmarkPortal.com and click on the RealityCheck™ logo or for more information call 805.614.0123 Ext. 77.

2. Peer Group Benchmark Subscription

Managers may want to a) see additional metrics that are specific to their sector; and b) know that the peer group is composed of their direct competitors. BenchmarkPortal is the trusted research organization that collects the additional data from all parties and produces the sector-specific report. ONLY anonymous and aggregate data are included as peer information in the reports.

Recommended for: Operations that are part of an identifiable competitive peer sector and that have key performance metrics that are specific to that sector.

For more information call 805.614.0123 Ext. 77.

3. Call Center Certification

Contact center leaders who want their centers to be certified as a Center of Excellence have urged us to develop this program, which utilizes our database, expertise and proprietary performance indices.

Recommended for:

- All contact centers that strive to achieve maximum effectiveness and efficiency
- Best practices organizations
- Outsourcers
- Multinationals wishing to instill best-practices globally

Center of Excellence
Your Call Center Name

has surpassed all the criteria required to be fully certified as a quality
call center providing a balance between efficient and effective service.
Certification is based on superior performance, as benchmarked by data from:

PURDUE UNIVERSITY
CENTER FOR CUSTOMER-DRIVEN QUALITY
WEST LAFAYETTE, INDIANA

DATE OF CERTIFICATION

Dr. Jon Anton

Benchmark Portal

For more information call: 805.614.0123 Ext. 61.

4. *Echo™* - Caller Satisfaction Measurement

'Every **C**ustomer **H**as **O**pinions...even if no one asks™'

> "With Echo, we now incorporate the 'voice of the customer' into everything we do. We love it."
> — Joyce Whalen, eBay Director of Customer Experience

BenchmarkPortal introduces **Echo**™, the ultimate service improvement solution—a groundbreaking new approach for translating direct customer feedback into rich actionable business intelligence. **Echo**™ challenges the traditional approach to measuring and improving customer service. The status quo has consistently fallen short of delivering the kind of results that create and maintain loyal customers. Based on our research, we have taken the best practices of the most successful companies and incorporated them into a dynamic closed-loop approach that really delivers.

Do more than just capture customer opinion. Use it.

Over 93% of companies say they collect customer opinions. Unfortunately...

Do you collect customer opinions?

No 7%
Yes 93%

67% of those companies don't use the opinions to influence internal change.

Do you use the customer opinions collected to influence internal change?

No 67%
Yes 33%

Echo™ provides an all-in-one solution:

- Scientifically-based customer feedback collection
- Primary source for monitoring agent effectiveness
- Service recovery, including post-recovery effectiveness measurement
- Core cause determination and analysis
- Effective, behavior-based agent coaching
- Meaningful metrics to track results
- Real-time Reporting
- Business intelligence needed to make informed decisions

The customer feedback collection component of **Echo**™ may be purchased as a stand-alone tool. However, we recommend the full **Echo**™ product as your ultimate service solution. We can help you develop and implement our revolutionary monitoring and coaching approach without loss of precious time in confronting technology and implementation issues. In most cases, we can launch **Echo**™ in just 60 days.

Recommended for: All contact centers that are interested in leveraging customer feedback to improve customer satisfaction.

For more information call: 805.614.0123 Ext. 62.

5. FairCompare™ Agent Satisfaction Benchmarking

 Finally, BenchmarkPortal introduces a new benchmarking tool designed specifically for Contact Centers. This tool allows you to compare the satisfaction results of your Contact Center agents to the results of other Contact Center agents!

As a Contact Center Professional, you know the importance of retaining your talent. Our **FairCompare**™ benchmarking surveys and reporting system quickly pinpoint areas of risk to proactively resolve them.

FairCompare™ lets you compare your Contact Center agents based on any category captured, including:

- Tenure
- Age-range
- Job Title
- Skill-set
- Supervisor
- And lots more!

FairCompare™ provides the ability to compare your Contact Center results to those of agents who've already participated in the survey. And when our database is sufficiently populated, you will also be able to compare your results to:

- Your Peer Group
- Your Industry
- Best-in-Industry
- Your Demographic Region
- Similar Environments

Customizable, always available, Online Reporting is a central feature of **FairCompare**™, providing results that you can act on quickly. Survey results help you pinpoint exact areas to focus on for immediate improvement initiatives, giving you the "Why" behind each "What."

Recommended for:
- Contact centers that are experiencing change management issues.
- Centers with high agent turnover rates.
- Centers that seek to be regarded as employers of choice.

For more information call: 805.614.0123 Ext. 63 or visit www.BenchmarkPortal.com and click on the FairCompare logo.

6. Benchmarking 201: Your Competitive Advantage

This NEW hands-on workshop is for all call center professionals who need a sound benchmark methodology to audit current performance results, then prioritize solutions toward achieving a competitive ROI. Participants will calculate the cause/cost of poor/excessive performance by case studies and quantify a 30-day impact plan. Attendees earn Certification as a Benchmark Specialist through Purdue University's Center for Customer-Driven Quality.

What Will I Learn?

- **Benchmarking the Difference**: Satisfaction, Retention, Operations, Cost containment

- **Competitive Performance**: Peer Reports, Gap analysis on effective/efficiency metrics

- **Solutions Savings**: Root Cause impact, Simulation charts, quantifiable action plan

Recommended for those who need a Peer-Industry Benchmark

For more information call: 805.614.0123 Ext. 65.

7. College of Call Center Excellence

The College of Call Center Excellence provides training courses that result in certification of contact center team members. Courseware is available for managers, supervisors and agents. Courses are taught both in-person and online. Some are taught in conjunction with BenchmarkPortal.

Recommended for: All centers. Training is a budget item for all centers that is rarely optimized. We can help you to get more for your training dollar.

For more information call: 805.614.0123 Ext. 64.

8. Industry Reports Available From BenchmarkPortal, Inc.

These industry reports contain hundreds of call center benchmarks and best practices for a specific industry:

Aerospace

Airline

All Industries

Automotive

Banking

Brokerage

Cable Television

Catalog

Computer Hardware

Computer Products

Computer Software

Credit Card

Financial Services

Government & Non-Profit

Healthcare Provider

Help Desk

Insurance

Insurance – Health

Insurance – Life

Insurance – Property & Casualty

Outbound Teleservices

Publishing & Media

Retail

Technical Support

Telecommunications

Transportation

Travel & Hospitality

Utilities

Wireless

Telecommunications
Industry Benchmark Report
Best-in-Class Call Center Performance

Principal Investigator
Dr. Jon Anton
Purdue University
Center for Customer-Driven Quality

Benchmark Portal
A Consortium of
Best Practices

Secure online ordering is available at:
www.BenchmarkPortal.com/bookstore or for more information call:
805.614.0123 Ext. 21.

9. Best Practice Reports

The team of researchers from BenchmarkPortal and Purdue University's Center for Customer-Driven Quality are turning their focus to your most vital resource: **Your People**.

Best Practices in Quality Monitoring and Coaching

We are pleased to announce our Best Practices in Quality Monitoring and Coaching study. This report is the fruit of almost nine months of research and analysis by the team of experts headed by Dr. Jon Anton, of Purdue University's Center for Customer-Driven Quality.

This study involved over a dozen carefully-selected call centers of distinction. This is the first study of its kind and resulted in a work of extreme interest and insight.

Best Practices in Workforce Management

Highlights of the reports:

- Study Findings: What are the impact factors in best practice companies.
- Workforce Optimization Cycle and Components
- Forecasting and Scheduling Alternatives
- Workforce Management Roles & Responsibilities
- Workforce Management Metrics
- Developing Optimal Schedules

For more information on these reports, call: 805.614.0123 Ext. 21.

10. The Anton Press

The following pages contain a listing of our current books as well as an order form. Secure online ordering is available at www.BenchmarkPortal.com/bookstore.

Business Navigation

Only two centuries ago, early explorers (adventurous business executives of those bygone days) were guided primarily with a compass and celestial navigation using reference points like the North Star. Today's busy executive also needs guidance systems with just-in-time business intelligence to navigate through the challenges of locating, recruiting, keeping, and growing profitable customers. The Anton Press provides this navigational system through practical, how-to-do-it books for the modern day business executive.

For more information call: 805.614.0123 Ext. 21.

20:20 CRM A Visionary insight into unique customer contacts

The contact center is at the heart of many businesses today, and CRM initiatives are making customer contact even more critical to the health of every company. 20:20 CRM provides a strategic view of where businesses should be going with their customer contact operation, with practical examples of how to get there.

ISBN 0-9630464-5-4   *By: Dr. Jon Anton and Laurent Philonenko*   **Price: $24.95**

Benchmarking at its Best for Contact Centers

Done right, and done regularly, benchmarking provides improved work life, career advancement and substantially increased earnings on a consistent basis. This book is an essential manual for continuous improvement peer group benchmarking that shows convincingly why proper professionalism in today's environment requires benchmarking. Includes valuable information on how to benchmark through BenchmarkPortal and describes the latest products and processes to help you get the most from this crucial activity. Also addresses emerging best practices in key areas such as: customer satisfaction measurement and using the voice of the customer for monitoring and coaching, agent satisfaction measurement, as well as the new symbolic language for desktop software that will reduce the time of data entry and interpretation for your agents in the future.

ISBN 0-9719652-1-8   *By: Bruce Belfiore with Dr. Jon Anton*   **Price: $9.95**

Call Center Benchmarking "How 'good' is good enough?"

This "how to" book describes the essential steps of benchmarking a call center with other similar call centers, with an emphasis on "self assessment." The reader learns how to plan a benchmark, how to collect the correct performance data, how to analyze the data, and how to find improvement initiatives based on the findings.

ISBN 1-55753-215-X   *By: Dr. Jon Anton*   **Price: $39.95**

Call Center Performance Enhancement - Using Simulation and Modeling

This book provides its readers with an understanding about the role, value, and practical deployment of simulation - an exciting technology for the planning, management, and analysis of call centers. The book provides useful guidelines to call center analysts, managers, and consultants who may be investigating or are considering the use of simulation as a vehicle in their business to responsibly manage change.

ISBN 1-55753-182-X   *By: Jon Anton, Vivek Bapat, Bill Hall*   **Price: $48.95**

Contact Center Management "By the Numbers"

With the ever increasing complexity of multi-channel customer contact handling, it is significant that this book addresses the challenges of managing such a contact center comprised of customer service agents, documented workflow processes, and enabling technology. Integrated reporting of calls, e-mails, Web-chat, and Web self-service becomes key.

The authors have written a very practical guide to managing a customer contact center "by the numbers." In contrast to most other departments in a company, the contact center has a constant flow of available performance metrics that are critical for the manager to use in making real-time decisions. The challenge is always what action to take when the "numbers change," and what remedies are best suited for specific performance gaps.

ISBN 0-9761109-0-3   *By: Dr. Jon Anton and Kámal Webb*   **Price: $32.95**

Customer Obsession: Your Roadmap to Profitable CRM

Finally, here is a book that covers the complete "journey" of CRM implementation. Ad Nederlof and Dr. Jon Anton have done the near impossible: to position CRM in such a way that it makes practical sense to C-level executives. Beginning with the title of the book, "Customer Obsession," on through the last chapter, this book positions CRM for what it really is, namely, a complete change in corporate strategy, from the top down, that brings the customer into focus.

ISBN 0-9719652-0-X   *By: Ad Nederlof and Dr. Jon Anton*   **Price: $24.95**

Customer Relationship Management: The Bottom Line to Optimizing Your ROI
Customer Relationship Management recommends effective initiatives toward improving customer service and managing change. Creative methodologies are geared toward building relationships through customer-perceived value instruments, monitoring customer relationship indices, and changing the corporate culture and the way people work.
ISBN 0-13-099069-8   *By Dr. Jon Anton and Natalie L. Petouhoff* **Price: $33.33**

Customer Relationship Management Technology: Building the Infrastructure for Customer Collaboration
From our research on the American consumer, it has become very clear that potentially the best customer service strategy is "to offer every possible channel for the customer to help themselves, i.e., self-service." Customer actuated service is mostly driven by technology, and the "art" of self-service is to ensure that the technology is intuitive, easy to use, and that the customer is rewarded for "having done the job themselves." This book delves into all the technology solutions that enable self-service. The reader will find a robust description of the technology alternatives, and many examples of how self-service is saving companies money, while at the same time satisfying customers.
ISBN 0-9630464-7-0   *By Dr. Jon Anton and Bob Vilsoet* **Price: $39.99**

Customer Service and the Human Experience: We, the People, Make the Difference
One of the leading challenges for today's managers is the training and motivating of excellent agents. While much attention has been focused on the technology and benefits of providing multiple channels for customer contact, little attention has been paid to handling the human part of the equation—training CSRs to field more than just telephone communications. Great statistics and benchmarking help the customer service/call center professional keep ahead of the ever-changing business environment as the authors successfully blend the critical human aspect of the center with the ever growing need for metrics and the bottom line.
ISBN 0-9719652-7-7   *By Dr. Rosanne D'Ausilio and Dr. Jon Anton* **Price: $34.95**

Customer Service at a Crossroads: What You Do Next to Improve Performance Will Determine Your Company's Destiny
By consistently delivering information about products, services and information to customer service agents, based on their individual skill levels—at the right time in the right way, organizations are also delivering a consistent, clear understanding of corporate objectives and vision. The result: thousands of customer interactions that delight the customer and improve retention as well as corporate profitability. Optimizing agent performance can quickly deliver incredible returns beyond customer loyalty. That is what this book is all about.
ISBN 0-9719652-6-9   *By Matt McConnell and Dr. Jon Anton* **Price: $15.95**

e-Business Customer Service: The Need for Quality Assessment
With the advent of e-business technology, we suddenly find ourselves with completely different customer service channels. The old paradigms are gone forever. This books details how to measure and manage e-business customer service. The book describes the key performance indicators for these new channels, and it describes how to manage by these new rules of engagement with specific metrics. Managing customer service in this "new age" is different, it is challenging, and it is impossible to migrate from the old to the new without reading this book.
ISBN 0-9630464-9-7   *By Dr. Jon Anton and Michael Hoeck* **Price: $44.00**

From Cost to Profit Center: How Technology Enables the Difference
This book is a series of case studies in which we collected performance metrics before and after implementation of specific technology solutions for call centers. In each case study we saw varying levels of improvement, and were then able to quantify the financial impact in terms of ROS, and in some cases, in terms of earnings per share. For call center managers contemplating the addition of new call center technology, this book will be an asset in better understanding the impact of technology in enabling higher performance.
ISBN 0-9719652-8-5   *By Dr. Jon Anton and R. Scott Davis*   **Price: $44.95**

How to Conduct a Call Center Performance Audit: A to Z
Call centers are an important company asset, but also a very expensive one. By learning to conduct a performance audit, readers will be able to understand over fifty specific aspects of a call center that must be running smoothly in order to achieve maximum performance in both efficiency and effectiveness of handling inbound customer calls.
ISBN 0-9630464-6-2   *By Dr. Jon Anton and Dru Phelps*   **Price: $34.99**

Integrating People with Process and Technology: Gaining Employee Acceptance of Technology Initiatives
This book contains valuable information regarding the "people" side of technology initiatives. Many companies buy the best hardware and software, and spend thousands of dollars implementing technology only to find out that the employees resist the changes, and do not fully adopt the new, and possibly, improved processes. By understanding how to manage people during change, managers will see a much quicker ROI on their technology initiatives.
ISBN 0-9630464-3-8   *By Jon Anton, Natalie Petouhoff, & Lisa Schwartz*   **Price: $39.99**

Listening to the Voice of the Customer
With the help of this book, the professional skills you need to measure customer satisfaction will lead you to different approaches until you have found the one that best fits you, your company, and your organization's culture.
ISBN 0-915910-43-8   *By Dr. Jon Anton*   **Price: $33.95**

Managing Web-Based Customer Experiences: Self-Service Integrated with Assisted-Service
The time to grow your call center into a multi-channel customer contact center is now. This book has the power to help you increase customer satisfaction through the implementation of Web self-service. The value of this book can be calculated in terms of calls deflected from your call center, increased customer retention, an ultimately in a healthy return on your investment. In this book, the authors take you step-by-step through the best practices that lead to a successful self and assisted-service strategy.
ISBN 0-9719652-4-2   *By Dr. Jon Anton and Mike Murphy*   **Price: $35.95**

Marketing Sucks! (and Sales, Too!)
Time-and-time again, great ideas become less effective, the marketing department's efficiency is diminished, there is the constant finger-pointing between sales and marketing, and presidents, CEOs, and others are frustrated over revenue goals that continue to go unmet. *Marketing Sucks! (and Sales, Too!)* captures the frustration felt by many parts of the organization when marketing and sales are not aligned. There is a better way. The authors write from direct experience. When your marketing and sales teams are aligned (on the same page) your bottom-line results will improve exponentially. These improved results can create a positive, perceptible shift in your company's finances and mood that will be valued in the boardroom, in the trenches, and ultimately, by your customer.
ISBN 0-9630464-4-6   *By Fred Janssen, Tom Marx and Tom Herndon*   **Price: $25.99**

Minimizing Agent Turnover: The Biggest Challenge for Customer Contact Centers

Some agent turnover can be functional, but most turnover is dysfunctional and can be very expensive. This book explores the types of turnover, including internal versus external; and documents the typical causes of agent turnover. Most importantly, this book describes a methodology for diagnosing the root causes of your agent turnover, and suggests improvement initiatives to minimize agent turnover at your customer contact center.

ISBN 0-9630464-2-X *By Dr. Jon Anton and Anita Rockwell* **Price: $39.99**

Offshore Outsourcing Opportunities

For call center executives wanting to explore and understand the benefits of offshore outsourcing, the authors have brought together 'under one cover' a comprehensive guide that takes the reader through each step of the complex issues of outsourcing customer service telephone calls to agents in another country. With the pressure of today's competitive climate forcing companies to take a hard look at providing higher quality customer services at lower costs, this book is a "must read" for every call center executive.

ISBN 0-9719652-3-4 *By Dr. Jon Anton and John Chatterley* **Price: $34.99**

Optimizing Outbound Calling: The Strategic Use of Predictive Dialers

The content of the book is organized in such a way as to assist the reader in understanding the complete end-to-end process of automated outbound call dialing. Specifically, the reader will find the following steps described in detail: a) preparing a needs assessment, b) selecting and contracting a predictive dialer supplier, c) implementing a predictive dialer solution, d) applying change management principles to ensure "buy-in" by existing agents, d) handling and using dialer reports, and finally, e) benchmarking dialer improvements to ensure attaining the anticipated ROI.

ISBN 0-9719652-2-6 *By Jon Anton and Alex G. Demczak* **Price: $39.99**

Selecting a Teleservices Partner: Sales, Service, and Support

This book tackles one of today's hottest topics: Customer Contact Outsourcing. Companies are in a quandary about the myriad of teleservices questions they're faced with, such as deciding to outsource, cost / benefit analysis, RFP development, proposal assessment, vendor selection, contractual requirements, service level performance measurement, and managing an ongoing teleservices relationship. With the authors help, readers will find this complex issue straightforward to approach, understand, and implement.

ISBN 0-9630464-8-9 *By Jon Anton and Lori Carr* **Price: $34.99**

The Four-Minute Customer: Getting Jazzed about Your People and Quality Management in Your Call Center

This is a very unique book directed at developing and maintaining "Top Reps" that are uniquely motivated to deliver the highest possible quality of caller customer service at your center. Learn what it takes to find and lead the best of the best. Don't settle for mediocrity. Instead, learn how to manage the best in class customer contact center by attracting and keeping Top Reps at your organization.

ISBN 0-9630464-1-1 *By Michael Tamer* **Price: $34.99**

Wake Up Your Call Center: Humanizing Your Interaction Hub, 3rd edition

With new and up-to-date material, this third edition speaks volumes about the need to reinforce the human element in the equation. This is a straight forward guide for humanizing the impersonal, with practical to-do's, real life examples, and applications to delight your customers. In depth chapters include mixed messages, change and stress management, conflict resolution, rapport building, and communicating powerfully, just to mention a few.

ISBN 1-55753-217-6 *By Rosanne D'Ausilio, Ph.D* **Price: $44.95**